Monument Eternal

FRANYA J. BERKMAN

Monument Eternal

THE MUSIC OF ALICE COLTRANE

WESLEYAN UNIVERSITY PRESS
Middletown, Connecticut

Wesleyan University Press
Middletown CT 06459
www.wesleyan.edu/wespress

Manufactured in the United States of America

Library of Congress Cataloging-in-Publication Data

Berkman, Franya J.
Monument eternal : the music of Alice Coltrane / Franya J. Berkman.
p. cm.—(Music/culture)
Includes bibliographical references and index.
ISBN 978-0-8195-6924-0 (cloth : alk. paper)—
ISBN 978-0-8195-6925-7 (pbk : alk. paper)
1. Coltrane-Turiyasangitananda, A. (Alice) 2. Pianists—United States—Biography. 3. Spiritual life—Hinduism. I. Title.
ML417.C746B47 2010
786.2092—dc22 2010016656
[B]

We gratefully acknowledge the assistance of the AMS 75 PAYS Endowment of the American Musicological Society.

To my mother, Lisa,
and my daughter, Sadie

Contents

Preface

In Search of Divine Songs

My first exposure to the music of Alice Coltrane occurred while I was relaxing in *savasana*, or the corpse pose, on the floor of a Brooklyn yoga studio in the winter of 1993. The instructor started the cassette player, and out came the rich sound of a black woman's tenor voice chanting the name of Siva, accompanied by a Wurlitzer organ and a small violin section. The music expressed an unusual combination of peace and longing. It was penetrating, soulful, and unlike anything I had ever heard. After class, I asked the instructor for the name of the artist. "Alice Coltrane, *Divine Songs,*" she answered. "Alice who?" I asked. "Coltrane," she replied. "Coltrane—like John Coltrane?" I inquired. "Yes, his wife," she confirmed.

For weeks, I searched intently for Alice Coltrane's music but could find nothing in any of the major record stores in Manhattan. My instructor kindly made me a cassette copy of *Divine Songs*, which I listened to regularly until I loaned it to a friend, who lost it. I had nearly forgotten about Alice Coltrane when, seven years later, I found two of her old LPs, *Journey in Satchidananda* and *Radha Krsna Nama Sankirtana*, in a colleague's extensive record collection. I listened again to this singular musician. In addition to Alice Coltrane's piano and harp improvisations, these recordings featured Pharoah Sanders's soprano saxophone, the hypnotic drone of the tamboura, and what sounded like a gospel choir singing the praises of Krishna. I was reminded of the Siva chant I had heard, and I began searching anew for her music.

At that time, I was a graduate student in ethnomusicology at Wesleyan University, and I examined discographies, jazz dictionaries, databases, and the World Wide Web. In the process, I learned that Alice Coltrane had played piano with her husband, John Coltrane, in the last years of his life.

Additionally, I discovered that Alice Coltrane had recorded over twenty-five jazz albums as either a leader or side person during the late 1960s and 1970s, working with many of the top names in jazz. I also learned that, with the exception of two or three articles, nothing of substance had been written about her. With the help of friends, I began painstakingly to collect all of her out-of-print recordings. But, alas, I found no *Divine Songs.*

At the time, I had been considering writing my dissertation about female jazz composers. However, after discovering the breadth of Alice Coltrane's music, and contentiously conferring with my friend, who insisted that I write about her, I decided that my doctoral thesis would focus on Alice Coltrane. But it was clear that I faced a huge obstacle. During my initial inquiries, I had learned that Alice Coltrane had become a spiritual recluse in the mid-1970s. She had founded an alternative religious community in Southern California, the Vedantic Center's Sai Anantam Ashram, and her intermediaries claimed that she did not grant interviews.

Stubbornly hoping to meet her, I traveled to Sai Anantam Ashram, intending to participate in one of their Sunday services open to the public. To my disappointment, Alice Coltrane—or Swamini Turiyasangitananda, as she was called, using the feminine form of "swami"—did not lead the prayers and *bhajans* (Hindu hymns) that day. Nonetheless, I found myself in a temple, sitting on the floor with a group of African American devotees of Sathya Sai Baba, an Indian guru, and singing what sounded like black music from a sanctified church. After a full hour of ecstatic song and brief closing remarks, I was invited to drink some iced tea and visit the bookstore. There I finally found a recording of *Divine Songs* displayed with Alice Coltrane's more recent devotional recordings and the spiritual texts she had written. I left with my arms full of her current music, her religious treatises, and more questions than answers.

That was nearly ten years ago, and much has happened since. The summer after my initial visit to Sai Anantam Ashram, Ms. Coltrane graciously granted me an extensive interview, which provided much of the groundwork for this study. I completed my dissertation about her music in 2003 and took a job as a music professor in Portland, Oregon, the same year; then I got married, gave birth to two children—who are now two and three years old—and somehow managed to complete this book before my tenure review. Busy with final revisions to the book, distracted by children, and immersed in my career, I received news that Alice Coltrane had passed away, quite unexpectedly.

I am very fortunate to have had the opportunity to meet Ms. Coltrane, not only because her life's work is rich and remarkable, but also because so many musicians of her generation are passing on now, and they have so much to teach us. I also feel especially lucky that, amid institutional commitments and the scholarly hurdles involved with getting my first academic book to press, Alice Coltrane continues to inspire me, both spiritually and musically. As I grow as a musician, I find her aesthetic choices increasingly interesting. As I aspire to be more humane and compassionate, her spiritual teachings offer me wisdom. As I journey into motherhood and learn how to be a mentor to college students, her shining example of equanimity and clarity in the face of obstacles and multiple responsibilities offers proof that everything can all be accomplished with grace and passion.

Acknowledgments

Many people have helped me bring this project to fruition, and I offer them my sincere gratitude. Most of all, I thank the late Alice Coltrane and her associates (George Bohannon, Terry Gibbs, Bennie Maupin, Cecil McBee, Ed Michel, Ben Riley, and Vishnu Wood) and members of the Sai Anantam Ashram community (in particular, Radha Reyes-Botafasina and Surya Botafasina) who took the time to speak with me at length.

Many others have also helped facilitate my research: my dissertation committee (Anthony Braxton, Ingrid Monson, Mark Slobin, and Su Zheng) and Deborah Nelson helped shepherd me through the early stages of this project; and other musicians, writers, and spiritual seekers interested in the topic assisted me as a graduate student (Shanti Norris and the staff of Integral Yoga; the jazz scholars Lars Bjorn, Eric Charry, Jim Gallert, Lewis Porter, and Steve Rowland; Dolores Brandon; the vibraphonist, and my friend, Jay Hoggard; and Shubalananda). Thanks are also owed to my ethnomusicologist friends who sustained me with their expertise, love, humor, inspiring conversation, and draft reading: Richard Harper, Michael Heffley, Hankus Netsky, and Michael Veal. More recently, Sherrie Tucker and George Lewis have offered valuable critiques in their readers' reviews for Wesleyan University Press.

I would also like to thank my Portland network at Lewis & Clark College and the new friends who have sustained me; Elise Gautier, my copy editor; and my immediate and extended family, who have kept my children safe, sound, creatively engaged, and lavished with love while I have taken the time to write this book—Grandma Sandy, Uncle Mike, Donna and Grandpa Frank, Shayla Holmes, Rashelle Chase, Aline Ochun, and my patient and devoted husband, Kristopher Logan Wallsmith.

Monument Eternal

INTRODUCTION

Alice Coltrane as Turiyasangitananda

As it was in the beginning, let your music forevermore be an expression of My Divinity in a sound incarnation of Myself as *nadabrahma*. For, eternally, divine music shall always be the sound of peace, the sound of love, the sound of life, and the sound of bliss.

—Alice Coltrane, *Endless Wisdom I*

To reach Sai Anantam Ashram, home of Alice Coltrane's Vedantic Center, you must travel on Triunfo Canyon Road, which goes through a lovely mountain pass in Agoura Hills, California, and winds leisurely between horse farms and exclusive homes in the Santa Monica Mountains. When you reach the ashram's entrance—a humble gate that is easily overlooked—music of Alice Coltrane and her devotees emanates from speakers set beside the dirt driveway. Entering the grounds, you find yourself in a small, protected valley, originally the sacred land of the Chumash Native Americans.

The ashram's stunning *mandir*, or temple, rises white as a cloud against the hills. In winter and spring, a brook in front of the temple splashes along, joining a tireless chorus of insects and birds. Several modest homes are set back into the hillside. Ashram inhabitants and visitors—mostly African American men, women, and children—are dressed in South-Asian attire: the women wear saris, the men kurtas. Speaking quietly among each other and greeting Sunday guests, they make their way with visitors to the steps of the *mandir*, remove their shoes, and enter the sanctum, men turning to the left and women to the right. The interior of the temple is simple and unadorned: there is a guest book and basket of hymnals by the entrance, a stretch of blue carpet and yellow cushions on the floor, and a small organ at the far end. Behind the organ stand two life-size posters of Sathya Sai Baba. On the right, out of sight, is a raised altar bearing an oil lamp, flowers, fruit, and images of Hindu deities. Once inside, the members of the small congregation silently sit down on the floor.

If you had the good fortune of attending Sunday services when the ashram's guru, Alice Coltrane—known in this context as Swamini Turiyasangitananda—was still alive, you would have seen her arrive dressed in orange robes, and flanked by attendants. She would make offerings at the altar, take her seat behind the Hammond B3 organ, and begin to play. First would be a *bhajan* to Ganesha, the elephant deity to whom Hindus traditionally pray before starting any religious and worldly endeavor. Alice would depress the pedals, and the bass vibrations would pass through the walls and floorboards. Playing syncopated chords with her left hand and a soaring, pentatonic melody with her right, she would signal the song leader in the men's section to start the men singing. The women would respond, and blues-inflected devotional music would fill the room. The hymn would have several tempo increases, propelled by Alice's dramatic modulations and the driving bass lines she would play with her feet. The congregation would create harmonies and counterpoint, and cry and shout in response to members' musical and emotional outpourings. They would clap ecstatically, and join in with tambourines and other hand-held percussion instruments. Their guru would smile and nod in rhythm, acknowledging the moment.

The *bhajans* that followed would be livelier, praising other deities of the Hindu pantheon: Rama, Krishna, Siva. Each hymn would have an extended and improvisational refrain section—similar to the Watts hymns one might hear sung by a Southern black congregation—in which individuals "inject the spirit of their being," as one member described it to me (Botafasina 2001). After the collective improvisation of the refrain, the hymn melody would return, and the *bhajan* conclude. Immediately, another would begin—with no announcements or conversations in between—and the organ would start again. To end the musical portion of the service, which lasted roughly an hour, the final hymn in praise of Sathya Sai Baba, "O Bhagavan," would be sung, following by closing prayers.

What kind of music is this? *Bhajans* at Sai Anantam Ashram are clearly sui generis. While it is common today to hear white Americans singing Indian devotional hymns at yoga centers and at concerts—American artists such as Krishna Das and Jai Utal have major record deals these days, and tickets to hear them sing cost twenty dollars or more—Alice Coltrane's *bhajans* are noncommercial, free to the public, and performed in a predominantly African American, gospel style. Furthermore, for nearly three decades they were played by Alice herself, who infused her arrangements with the diverse genres she explored over the course of her life as a church accompanist, bebop pianist, composer, and avant-garde improviser.

What's more, the ritual that one finds at Alice's ashram reflects her own iconoclastic musical and spiritual journey. In the *mandir*, she reproduced the aesthetics of black sacred music characteristic of her formative years in Detroit. She also maintained an approach to musical worship that reflects the theory of her late husband, John Coltrane, that music has a universal, transcendent nature—a theory she synthesized with elements of Hindu practice learned from her gurus and in her travels to India. And remarkably, although this musical worship at Sai Anantam Ashram clearly recapitulates her own evolution, it has become a ritual separate from any notion of her as an artist. Ashram members do not experience *bhajans* as if they are performing the compositions of Alice Coltrane. They believe, as their beloved swamini did, that "chanting is a universal devotional engagement, one that allows the chanter to soar to higher realms of spiritual consciousness. Chanting is a healing force for good in our world, and also in the astral worlds. Chanting can bring a person closer to God because that person is calling on the Lord" (http://www.saiquest.com December 2007).

How do we make sense of these songs? They are at once African American and South Asian. Their histories can be traced to religious revivals spanning India's medieval period, as well to cultural formations that coalesced in the New World among the descendants of African slaves. They form a genre attributable to an individual composer, yet they are also a ritual that belongs to the whole community. Appreciating and understanding Alice Coltrane's sacred music at the ashram—and, for that matter, the other music that she recorded and performed over the course of her prolific career—requires that we move beyond reified categories of musical style and religious practice and honor the open-ended quality of cultural production and the ways we pass on the life of cultures. Most importantly, it draws our attention to the formidable role of Alice Coltrane—a woman often relegated to the footnotes of works about her late husband—as both musician and guru.

It may seem odd to begin a book about Alice Coltrane, a jazz icon, by describing her role at Sai Anantam Ashram. The reader probably expects this first part of the book to detail her early musical experiences in a chronological manner, consistent with most jazz biographies. But this is not a jazz biography; rather, it is an exploration of the music of a woman and devotional musician whose contributions transcend such genre-specific constraints. Understanding Alice Coltrane's superior artistry and her religious music expands the definition of jazz and challenges the process of canonization. It also provides an opportunity to discuss experimental music created by black composers and the phenomena of musical and spiritual hybridity in the late twentieth century on a broader scale. For lack of a single, concise term, this study of Alice Coltrane is best described as an ethnomusicological life history that prioritizes the role of spirituality in her musical aesthetics and in the cultural spaces she inhabited.

Alice Who?

Few people in the music business are aware of Alice Coltrane's role as guru or of her musical ministry. She is known primarily as a jazz pianist and harpist, or simply as the widow of the legendary saxophonist and composer John Coltrane. Among jazz aficionados, her importance tends to rest on the controversial role she assumed when she replaced McCoy Tyner as the pianist in her husband's last rhythm section. Accordingly, her important works are seldom considered to exceed the small body of recordings she made with John Coltrane during the last year of his life. Few people are aware, then, of the Hindu-influenced devotional music she composed and arranged with her devotees, despite the current popularity of music for yoga and meditation. Fewer still know that by the mid-1970s, her works included more than twenty albums of original compositions and virtuoso improvisations, which she recorded for the Impulse and Warner Brothers labels with some of the giants of modal and free jazz—Pharoah Sanders, Leroy Jenkins, Rashied Ali, Roy Haynes, Cecil McBee, Reggie Workman, and Ron Carter—as her sidemen. Even more obscure are her formative, pre-Coltrane years in Detroit when, as Alice Mcleod, bebop virtuoso, she performed in the company of the Motor City's extraordinary postwar pianists: Barry Harris, Terry Pollard, Hank Jones, Tommy Flanagan, and Sir Roland Hanna, to name only a few.

Alice's musicianship, like that of many of John Coltrane's sidemen, has been overshadowed by the contributions of the man many consider to be the last great innovator of modern jazz.[1] One also wonders whether her avant-garde experiments would have received any attention at all had she lacked the Coltrane name, particularly given that her continually expanding musical conception, which coalesced in the hybrid ritual music of the ashram, fell outside conventional definitions of jazz or any other identifiable single genre. After her teen years as a church pianist during the late 1940s and early 1950s, she played and composed in a variety of musical styles: gospel, bebop, rhythm and blues, Western classical, free jazz, and Indian devotional. Her albums feature original compositions for standard jazz instrumentation—bass, drums, piano—as well as works for harp, Wurlitzer organ, strings, and choir. She adapted the works of Stravinsky, Dvorak, and her late husband. She also recorded herself singing and playing her own version of ancient Indian chants and hymns. Yet for marketing reasons, or by association with her husband, Alice Coltrane is classified as a jazz musician, although she herself did not call her music jazz—she believed she played "spiritual music" (interview with author, 2001).

For better or worse, Alice experienced the fate of many exceptionally talented women married to men recognized for their brilliance: while her own contributions received attention, she never really got a fair shake. During the late 1960s, many of John Coltrane's fans viewed her as an accomplice to the so-called anti-jazz experiments of his final years. Her notoriety was further exacerbated by the tremendous power she assumed when she took control of Jowcol Music, her husband's publishing company, and decided the fate of his unreleased materials after his death. In particular, her choice to overdub her own playing on his signature recording of "My Favorite Things" angered many in the jazz establishment.

While Alice's eccentricities and her role as the wife of a legendary musician surely contributed to the marginal, if not contested, status of her own music, other discursive forces also played a significant part. As subjects of study, black female musicians have been quintessential others, either overlooked because of—or overdetermined by—the categories of gender, race, and class. To a great extent, social constructions of difference burden black male musicians as well: their lives are routinely viewed in light of the pervasive challenges of racial discrimination they encounter, and whether they represent their group as "race men." However, compared to black male musicians, black female musicians rarely transcend difference and obtain the status of artist. Even in the noblest attempts to explore the music and lives of black female musicians, scholars have tended to focus on personal hardships and identity politics. Few have challenged "the current romanticization of the black subject and the refusal of complexity in the representation of the lives of black women," and even fewer have focused adequately on their music (Carby 1992, 178).

When women instrumentalists have garnered attention for their talents in the male-dominated jazz world, their success has usually hinged on the supposedly male qualities of their playing: they are praised for their strong rhythm, big sound, and aggressive improvisations. Conversely, when a woman plays sensitively or with quiet dynamics, her musicianship tends to be dismissed for lacking sufficient masculine characteristics. This gendered mediation is evident everywhere in the assessment of Alice's solo career. Critics who expected to find the aggressive intensity that characterized her work with John Coltrane's ensemble were frequently disappointed. For instance, in his *Down Beat* review of her 1970 release, *Ptah the El Daoud*, Ed Cole wrote: "It seems incredible that a group so heavily stamped by the late John Coltrane would not be able to pull off an album, but that's just what happens here. It's not that this is not good music, because it is, but it doesn't come close to the potential of the individual players. It seems that each subdued his talents to accommodate the others" (1971, 20). In his review of *A Monastic Trio* (1968), John Litweiler commented: "the harp side of this LP presents waves of sound, a wispy impressionist feeling without urgent substance" (1969, 22). Ekkehard Jost asserted that "Alice Coltrane is not a 'hard' pianist who drives the music with rhythmic accentuations" (1974, 98).

Listeners also tend to equate musical characteristics such as loud dynamics and jarring timbral effects with the counterculture and political resistance, especially during the 1960s, when such explorations were still novel. As a result, Alice's more intimate albums from the late 1960s did not have the palpable political innuendo that one could feel in the music of her avant-garde colleagues. She may indeed have lost some of her avant-garde audience by 1970, at least those louder-is-better "free-jazz" fans who were unaware of her aggressive approach in albums such as *Universal Consciousness* (1971) and *Transfiguration* (1978). Alice's seemingly apolitical choices have also placed her at odds with the models of resistance and radicalism that black women of historical importance typically embody.[2] Although during the height of the civil rights movement she was playing dissonant, freely improvised jazz—a style that tends to be associated with cultural nationalism and black militancy—she opted not to engage in a direct or public manner with "the struggle." She was not a song leader or educator such as Bernice Johnson Reagon,[3] who used black spirituals to effect social change. Nor was she politically outspoken like Abbey Lincoln or Nina Simone. Gentle in demeanor, a devoted wife and mother of four, Alice's persona was, in many respects, consistent with the patriarchal helpmate image that the revolution espoused, an image that has since been scrutinized by black feminist theorists.[4]

While Alice conformed in her domesticity to this conservative aspect of black liberation ideology in the 1960s, her universalist views ultimately challenged many of the Afrocentric tenets of black liberation popular at the time. In her writing and interviews, she consistently expressed the importance of transcending category and limitation. Beginning in the late 1960s, she expressed belief in a transcendent oneness, a "universal consciousness" that subsumes all creativity and religious faith. Despite the ostensible forms of ethnicity one finds in her devotional music and religious practices, cultural specificity and racial identity did not figure in her religious or creative philosophy. Her universalist views, therefore, were—and still are—at variance with those of musicians and scholars who make blackness or an African worldview central to African American cultural production.

Spiritual Aesthetics

A religious sensibility steadily guided Alice Coltrane's artistry—a feeling that music "had to come from the composer's heart and spirit and soul, not just his mind" (quoted in Lerner 1982, 23). This attitude, combined with her uncanny musical skills and an experimental temperament, led her along a path that was not only musically but spiritually daring. Compared to the conservative Christianity of her childhood in Detroit, Alice Coltrane was a religious maverick. During the late 1960s, she and her husband began to explore meditation and a universalist approach to religion. Their spiritual pursuits as a couple extended to the bandstand, where they played a personalized version of spiritual music in the form of dissonant, free-meter improvisation. After her husband's death in 1967, Alice experienced what she called a "reawakening." From that point on, her music either attempted to express her experience of the divine or was written and performed as an offering to God.

In 1969, she befriended the Indian guru Swami Satchidananda and discovered the philosophical and spiritual teachings of the Vedas. She was still raising her four children when she recorded the majority of her albums, which, like John Coltrane's *A Love Supreme* (1965), included extensive liner notes that testified to her personal transformation. The albums feature devotional compositions and improvisations that increasingly drew on both free-jazz idioms and the *bhajans* that she discovered on her pilgrimages to India, as well as semi-orchestrated works and harp pieces reflecting her deepening mysticism.

In 1976, she had a revelation in which she was instructed to become a Hindu swami. She had founded the Vedantic Center in 1972, and in 1983, after she had joined the monastic order, she established Shanti Anantam Ashram, later renamed Sai Anantam Ashram. She served as spiritual director for the ashram and regularly played for services and delivered sermons until her passing on January 12, 2007. After a long hiatus from public performance, interrupted only periodically by benefit concerts in honor of her late husband, she returned to touring in the last years of her life, playing with a jazz quartet featuring her son, the tenor saxophone player Ravi Coltrane, and her former bassists, Reggie Workman and Charlie Haden.

During her monastic period, she wrote four little-known spiritual treatises—*Monument Eternal* (1977), *Endless Wisdom I* (1981), *Divine Revelations* (1995), and *Endless Wisdom II* (1999)—all of which were published by her own Avatar Book Institute. *Monument Eternal* documents her spiritual rebirth from 1968 to 1970. As she described the work in its preface, it is "a book based upon the soul's realizations in Absolute Consciousness and its spiritual relationships with the Supreme One." The two volumes of *Endless Wisdom* make up a comprehensive treatise that explores the nature of the divine and the proper relationship between humanity and God. Here Alice claims no authorship; in the preface to the first volume, she explains that she was "divinely sanctioned" to "inscribe" the words of the Lord based on "sacred communications" (9). *Divine Revelations* is written in the form of a diary, with entries that document revelations between 1968 and 1995. Each entry recounts conversations that she had with avatars in the form of Rama and Krishna, or with the living guru Satya Sai Baba, whose followers consider him to be an embodiment of God.

As a self-proclaimed mystic and composer of devotional music, Alice might be compared to numerous Western art-music, jazz, and gospel musicians who have written sacred works. Several figures immediately come to mind: the medieval saint Hildegard of Bingen, the twentieth-century French composer Olivier Messiaen, Duke Ellington and Mary Lou Williams with their jazz masses, and Thomas Dorsey, who was "called" to compose his famous gospel song "Precious Lord." However, Alice's commitment to universal spirituality as a guiding principle and her use of wide-ranging religious and musical sources distinguish her from these other composers. In her liner notes and spiritual treatises, she employed mythic imagery from a host of religious traditions, including Christianity, Hinduism, Islam, Buddhism, and the religion of ancient Egypt. In a parallel fashion, her music brought together diverse musical styles and cultural traditions in an attempt to portray her experience of spiritual transformation and exaltation.

One might praise her for anticipating what is now the rather common postmodern trend of mixing and juxtaposing genres from vastly different historical periods and cultural traditions. However, her devotional compositions lack the oppositional irony typically associated with postmodern aesthetics. Rather, I suggest that it was her extraordinary religious experiences and her universal spiritual philosophy—infused by the Vedic notion that the paths are many, yet the destination one—that inspired her to draw from so many diverse sources in her musical composition and her written testimony.

As a devotional musician, Alice appropriated and synthesized numerous genres according to divine inspiration, using them as vehicles for meditation, ecstasy, praise, and worship. Her spiritual fervor granted her enormous artistic license, which has been a source of contention among critics and colleagues. This, coupled with her mystical claims, has made her rather suspect in the eyes of the neoconservative jazz establishment, and not without warrant.[5] Many devotional musicians emerged during the 1960s and 1970s. Some emulated John Coltrane, while others were swept up in the popularity of Eastern mysticism; still others profited from the market potential of the cosmic, exotic, and occult. Alice Coltrane, however, belongs in a category by herself. Her religious transfiguration during the era resulted in music of great emotional and artistic depth, as well as a lasting commitment to spiritual duties that ultimately took precedence over musical composition and performance altogether.

In assessing Alice's "spiritual music," one should also keep in mind that its hybrid nature is not uncommon in religious musical genres. Although they have not been studied comparatively, ecstatic musical traditions tend to appropriate an unusually wide array of source materials. For instance, the melodies of Hasidic *nigunim* (wordless devotional tunes) are frequently popular songs deemed sacred by a rabbi; some are even military marches.[6] Similarly, *bhajan* melodies in India have been lifted from famous film scores and then matched with religious texts; their widespread familiarity has made them ideal for communal song. This mode of secular cross-fertilization is also common in black Protestant music. Scholars have documented a process of constant exchange: though the texts and lyrics might change, the musical components of genres such as spirituals, gospel music, and the blues often sound indistinguishable.

The breadth of Alice Coltrane's music also results from the diversity of musical styles available to contemporary musicians and composers. In *Subcultural Sounds: Micromusics of the West*, Mark Slobin calls attention to the intricacy of musical exchange that occurs in late capitalist societies. For Slobin, "micromusics" result from a complex "web of affiliations" that individuals and groups encounter at the intersections of three types of cultural experience: the "supercultural," "subcultural," and "intercultural." "Supercultural" refers to coercive aspects of culture produced by large-scale social and political structures such as government and industry.[7] "Subcultural" refers not only to groups united by common factors such as ethnicity, class, and gender but also to more subtle, frequently flexible categories determined by individual choice and belonging. "Intercultural" refers to the complex exchange that occurs across the boundaries of a nation-state through "the commodified music system" or "the diasporic linkages that subcultures set up across national boundaries." Given this view of culture, Slobin argues, "we need to see music as coming from many places and moving along many levels of today's society, just as we have learned to think of groups and nations as volatile, mutable social substances rather than as fixed units for instant analysis. Yet at any moment, we can see music at work in rather specific ways, creating temporary force fields of desire, belonging, and, at times, transcendence" (1993, xiv).

An African American Spiritual Narrative

Even while her nonsectarian religious philosophy led her down extremely unconventional roads for an African American woman from her generation and fostered her avant-garde and hybrid musical aesthetics, Alice Coltrane always remained deeply connected to the African American spiritual and musical locus of her family's origins. If one looks beyond her surface eclecticism, it quickly becomes apparent that Alice's creative impulse was firmly rooted in time-honored forms of African American religious expression. Specifically, her collective works can be seen as a form of religious testimonial, or "testifyin'," a ritual act situated in the religious traditions of her youth.[8] As James Cone writes,

> Testifying is an integral part of black religious tradition. It is the occasion when the believer stands before the community of faith in order to give account of the hope that is in him or her. Although testimony is unquestionably personal and thus primarily an individual story, it is also a story accessible to those in the community of faith. Indeed the purpose of testimony is not only to strengthen an individual's faith but also to build a faith community. (Cone 1982, 14)

As a poetic and evocative frame for this study, I propose that Alice Coltrane's various forms of testifying—in both text and music—constitute a multidimensional, African American spiritual autobiography. I draw this broad parallel for a number of reasons, first and foremost because the confessional and autobiographical nature of her *oeuvre* invites this manner of interpretation. With a heartfelt message to her listeners in the liner notes of *A Monastic Trio* (1968), the first album she made after her husband's death, she began a lifelong and increasingly extensive narrative about her relationship with God and her own spiritual evolution: "unable to answer all of the wonderful cards and telegrams sent me during the summer of 1967, I would like to take this opportunity to say thank you, sincerely, on behalf of my family and myself, for your kindness." By 1971, she was prefacing each tune with an edifying message, a teaching, or an evocative description of the process of spiritual transformation. In her liner notes, she discussed how particular pieces were motivated by conversations she had during her meditations with the Lord and his emissaries, and how various compositions were written as offerings to God.

Valuable historical, sociopolitical, and literary connections can also be drawn between her own confessional statements and those found in African American spiritual autobiographies, past and present. Historically, spiritual autobiographies, particularly Protestant versions, have been written to "help initiate others into the experience" and to "teach, edify, persuade and exhort" (Brereton 1991, 3). In the hands of African American writers, the spiritual autobiography has also had a radical purpose. According to William L. Andrews, the African American spiritual autobiography has provided "a way of declaring oneself free, of redefining freedom and then assigning it to oneself in defiance of one's bonds to the past or to the social, political, and sometimes even moral exigencies of the present" (1986a, xi).

It is characterized by "the reconstructing of one's past in a meaningful and instructive form, the appropriating of empowering myths and models of the self from any available resource, and the redefining of one's place in the scheme of things by redefining the language used to locate one in that scheme" (7). Andrews also asserts that the history of black autobiography has been one of "increasingly free story telling." That is, "the journey of black autobiography toward free telling first had to pass through intervening consciousness of amanuenses and editors, then had to challenge generic conventions and discursive properties of writing itself, before finally undertaking the greatest task of all, the appropriation of language for purposes of signification outside that which was privileged by the dominant culture" (290). Alice's adventuresome and genre-defying qualities as a writer and musician function within this economy of "free telling" that Andrews describes.[9]

In many respects, Alice's example as a religious seeker and iconoclast is also similar to that of black female preachers from earlier eras—women such as Rebecca Jackson, who founded a small Shaker community of black women in the late nineteenth century; and the black matriarchs Sojourner Truth, Amanda Berry Smith, and Jerena Lee, who, as Alice Walker writes, were directed by "an inner-spirit" and "abandoned the early black churches to find a religious audience of their own" (Walker 1982, 79). And Alice's texts, like those of these black evangelical women writers from the eighteenth and nineteenth centuries, were inspired and sanctioned by what she believed were mystical experiences. Robert Ellwood—whose definition seems to best approach Alice's encounters and those of her evangelical sisters—describes a mystical experience as one that "in a religious context is immediately interpreted by the experiencer as direct, unmediated encounter with ultimate divine reality. This experience engenders a deep sense of unity and suggests that during the experience the experiencer was living on a level of being other than the ordinary" (Ellwood 1999, 39). Like Alice, Jarena Lee, Rebecca Jackson, and Julia Foote, among others, felt compelled by God to document their spiritual lives. Acting as amanuenses in their respective works—*The Religious Experience and Journal of Mrs. Jarena Lee* (1849), *Gifts of Power* (1871), *A Brand Plucked from the Fire: An Autobiographical Sketch* (1886)—they dictated their direct communications with the Lord and wrote about receiving divine gifts and powers.

To be even more precise, Alice's work embodies a unique form of mystically inspired text that Chanta M. Haywood has called "autometography," which is an autobiographical narrative that "reveals a subject's understanding of themselves that transcends earthly constructions of their lives and identities" (Haywood 2003, 116). Haywood uses this term to describe the writings from the nineteenth and early twentieth centuries of black female preachers who were similarly called to serve. She draws attention to the way in which the women's texts and personal examples not only offered hope of salvation, but also set forth a "god-inspired social critique" that challenged the social expectations of the day (17).[10] Describing autometography and the narrators' subject position, Haywood writes: "every aspect of their being was interpreted from a metaphysical vantage point that allowed them to see themselves as prophesying daughters, a perception that would in many ways require them to challenge nineteenth century notions of who they should be" (111). She states: "On the level of sociopolitical strategy, this religious conviction became a cultural passport, allowing the women access to physical and ideological spaces otherwise denied them . . . They presented a powerful challenge to dominant 19th century ideas about woman's proper space" (20).

While twentieth-century black women writers have not been required to stand behind God's authority in order to claim agency or their literary voices, the identification of a sacred self or soul and the unmediated relationship with God have nonetheless remained salient themes in the writings of contemporary African American women novelists, in both their autobiographies and their fiction. Scholars have explored how this trope has been recapitulated in the works of such literary figures as Alice Walker and Toni Morrison, among others.[11] Alice Coltrane, like these "womanist" writers[12] who emerged with her during the 1970s, appropriated this holy mantle of self-realization in order to address contemporary concerns.[13]

In the late 1960s and early 1970s, what were the social expectations for an African American jazz musician from Detroit, a Baptist woman from a conservative middle-class family, a mother of four? Surely Alice was not expected to become an avant-garde improviser, let alone a swamini. And whatever these expectations may have been, they must have been complicated by her position as a black public figure during a period of heightened racial tension and African American cultural nationalism—not to mention by the responsibility of being the widow of John Coltrane. Alice's personal and mystical relationship with the divine appears to have provided the direction and strength that she needed to transcend social expectations, skepticism, and criticism, and chart her own creative path. That relationship also ultimately paved the way for new possibilities of African American spiritual and musical identity. In a journal entry dated July 3, 1975, for instance, she wrote:

On this day, Lord Sri Rama said, "Several persons in this country (USA) are inquiring amongst themselves as to 'how does an American, black, Christian lady become an East Indian Swamini'?"

In this regard, Baba said, "it matters not whether public inquiry and opinion are favorable or unfavorable; one's country and nationality are of no underlying criterion. If one has dedicated his life in devotion to God, he can be selected to become a candidate for initiation into the renounced order of sanyas." (A. Coltrane 1995, 87)

Situating Alice boldly alongside these female preachers and womanist writers allows for a feminist reading of her life, in which the "interior spiritual resources" of black women in America are given the same attention as the stories of male-centered genius that typically dominate jazz biographies (Walker 1982, 79).

Alice's *oeuvre* also shares an inclusive aesthetic with the work of her evangelical predecessors; one can thus extend the hybridity arguments already made into the realm of African American spiritual narratives. As William Andrews and others argue, the African American spiritual autobiography has never had a standard form, poetics, or rhetorical style. During different periods in its evolution, black women writers drew from "whatever sources were available," calling upon a variety of "empowering myths" from multiple religious and folk traditions (Andrews 1986, 290). The very language they employed was multitextual: it borrowed from Protestant conversion narratives, the King James Bible, the sentimental novel, political petitions, and the vernacular. Writers also wrote poems and parables to describe their experiences, especially in their accounts of dreams and visions. While Alice's incorporation of terms and concepts from Hinduism are a radical departure from the writings of previous evangelical women, the breadth of religious references and the eclectic nature of her texts still unite her work with these earlier spiritual narratives.

On the one hand, the hybridity historically found in African American spiritual autobiographies results from the individual cultural experiences of the narrator, such as the educational opportunities she had, her exposure to other texts, prior religious background, and regional style. On the other hand, it also stems from the complex, often embattled subject position of the black woman narrator. Literary critics have theorized black female subjectivity along these lines and have posited that it implicitly produces texts of a hybrid nature. Mae Gwendolyn Henderson argues that "black women must speak in a plurality of voices as well as in a multiplicity of discourses. Through the multiple voices that enunciate her complex subjectivity, she not only speaks familiarly in the discourse of the other(s) but as Other she is in contestorial dialogue with the hegemonic dominant and subdominant or ambiguously (non)hegemonic discourses . . . these writers enter simultaneously into familial or *testimonial* and public, or competitive discourses—discourses that both affirm and challenge the values and expectations of the reader" (Henderson 1994, 264). Henderson borrows the term "speaking in tongues" to describe this phenomenon. She further distinguishes between glossolalia, which can be seen as a metaphor for the "private language" of the church community, and the Bakhtinian notion of heteroglossia, which pertains to "the multiple languages of public discourse" (118).

These hybridity arguments are relevant to Alice's works in a variety of ways. First, she clearly drew from "whatever sources were available." In her prose, she moved between disparate styles: poetry, first-person diary confessions, and the mystical direct writing of God's word. She borrowed liberally from the King James Bible, from translations of the Bhagavad Gita, and from her own colloquial speech. In a parallel fashion, her music synthesized gospel progressions, Western art music, and dissonant, free-meter improvisations. Alice produced a hybrid artistry that spoke in tongues. She uttered the insider, ritual tongue of glossolalia, drawing on the sacred and secular vernaculars of Detroit's African American subculture. She also spoke in the multiple public discourses of art music and jazz modernism. Her work achieved a complex synthesis that does, in Henderson's words, ultimately "both affirm and challenge the values and expectations of the reader" (118).

That said, her *oeuvre* moves completely beyond these binaries: her self-proclaimed mysticism disrupts these relational modes. In fact, I believe that Alice was trying to transcend the "complex subjectivity" that Henderson speaks of, and to do so required moving beyond the realm of the material world and its limits and conditions. This is why I find the word "autometography" relevant here. Alice's collective works and her personal example as a swami are best described as a spiritual narrative that reveals an understanding of herself that, as Haywood put it, "transcends earthly constructions."

The Spiritual as Political

Exploring Alice's spiritual music and her religious pursuits presents a substantial scholarly challenge. In the secular academy, spirituality has taken a back seat to the so-called important stories of political history. This is particularly evident in jazz studies. Even though many famous jazz musicians have acknowledged the role of religion in their creative processes, jazz scholars tend to focus on issues of black political oppression and have not yet productively engaged with religion. Both the irrationality associated with religion and the ecstatic and supposedly earthy qualities of black church music also conflict with the modernist intellectual agenda of "jazz uplift."[14] Furthermore, within the black community, the role of the church in African American culture has been contested territory and has inspired heated polemics; the church has been viewed both as a wellspring of authentic black culture and political empowerment and as a corrupt, backward institution representing the hegemonic forces of white society.

Nevertheless, this study is predicated on an exploration of the crucial role of spirituality in avant-garde jazz improvisation. Scholars who write about black music, particularly avant-garde jazz during the mid- to late 1960s, must contend, at least in some manner, with the social reality of black revolution. Two dominant and opposed methodologies have emerged in 1960s jazz scholarship. Unfortunately, neither has produced a vocabulary sufficient to describe the relationship among the creative process, spirituality, and politics. One method of scholarship separates the aesthetic from the political: its works customarily begin with a brief nod to the civil rights movement, followed by a hasty retreat into the musician's work.[15] The advantage of this method is that the black jazz musician, who has been overdetermined as a racial and political figure through decades of criticism, acquires the status of individual and genius. The disadvantage, of course, is the disavowal of revolutionary cultural shifts that shaped artistic production. The second scholarly method encodes the music with radical meaning. Writers in this camp tend to relate musical characteristics such as free rhythm, collective improvisation, and timbral intensity to cultural nationalism and black militancy.[16]

However, situating the explorations of 1960s jazz within a purely political framework is insufficient, particularly with respect to an artist like Alice Coltrane. Her music and commentary from the mid-1960s onward stressed the personal and the spiritual, not the political. I do not mean to suggest that the religious and political facets of culture ought to stand at oppositional poles. Rather, they should be viewed, in the words of Robert Ellwood, "as bands in a single spectrum" (Ellwood 1994, 9). Alice Coltrane's spiritual pursuits should not be posed against the political activism of the era and therefore overlooked. Her spiritual explorations should be seen as a creative, energizing, and productive alternative to more explicit forms of political protest—an alternative that may, indeed, have deeply radical implications.[17]

To shed light on the political nature of Alice's eclectic and Eastern-influenced spiritual music, I have contextualized her work within 1960s religious culture and the search for "a new spirituality" among members of the Black Arts movement (Neal 1989, 77). The cultural historian Melani McAlister has written persuasively on the political dimensions of African-Americans' interest in non-Western religions during the 1960s. She sees such spiritual explorations among black Americans as a way of forming "an alternative sacred geography" that provides "alternatives to official policy, framing transnational affiliations and claims to racial or religious authority that challenged the cultural logic of American power." In her view, these spiritual pursuits are part of a larger project that encompasses "a re-visioning of history and geography in order to construct a moral and spiritual basis for contemporary affiliations and identities" (McAlister 1999, 638).

An Ethnomusicology of the Individual

It should be clear by now that this is an interdisciplinary and culture-based musical study. To some extent, the cultural emphasis of this project has been a necessity due to Alice Coltrane's reclusive nature. The personal data that musical biographers gather for extensive narratives have not been available. Alice cherished her privacy. Thus, poring over letters, scrapbooks, diaries, and musical sketches, an activity enjoyed by most biographers, has not been possible. I did have the good fortune of meeting Alice Coltrane on several occasions and interviewing her. I also visited Sai Anantam Ashram and participated in services. To gather additional information, I spoke with her devotees, friends, colleagues, and producers and have examined statements she made to journalists and John Coltrane scholars, as well as an extensive, unedited interview she made for a radio documentary in the early 1980s about her musical career. I have also listened closely to her recorded music and to her public performances in recent years.

In chapter 1, I situate Alice Coltrane's formative musical experiences within the tight-knit musical networks of the African American community in Detroit. I place particular emphasis on her early training in the Baptist church and other black denominations, the historical presence of important African American musical families, and the unique jazz fraternity that fostered a thriving local bebop subculture. With this elucidating context in place, I conclude with an analysis of her little-known bebop recordings with the vibraphonist Terry Gibbs.

In chapter 2, I explore her musical development during her time as John Coltrane's musical, spiritual, and marital partner. I describe the process by which she came to absorb his unique aesthetic and spiritual philosophy. In addition to analyzing her playing in John Coltrane's late quintet, I discuss the changing nature of American religion during the 1960s, giving special emphasis to the new forms of spirituality that emerged among black Americans in the context of Black Power.

In chapter 3, I examine Alice's spiritual transformation after her husband's death, and its effects on her musical aesthetics during her solo career. Her *oeuvre*—eleven albums on the Impulse! and Warner Brothers labels—is viewed as the legacy of her early years in Detroit and the influence of her husband, and as a completely unique contribution to avant-garde jazz and world-music fusions of the late 1960s and 1970s. I ground her innovative musical approaches and the increasingly hybrid nature of her compositions in her experiences traveling with her guru, Swami Satchidananda, throughout India; her theory of musical transcendence; her commitment to a universal concept of spirituality; and her belief in the Vedantic notion of self-realization. Finally, in chapter 4, I explore her *bhajans*—the devotional music that currently serves as ritual music at Sai Anantam Ashram—in the context of a community that has followed her teachings for nearly thirty years.

My ethnomusicological and interdisciplinary approach as a scholar widens the boundaries and concerns that typify jazz biographies. Musicians participate in interpenetrating musical subcultures: those of family, church, ethnic group, school, neighborhood, city, region, musicians' collective, nightlife, and so forth. Mapping the life and music of Alice Coltrane in an ethnographic manner allows us to observe the musical continuities and discontinuities between these communities; it affords a means of elucidating the multiple cultural spaces she occupied. For instance, the story of Alice Coltrane's early years reveals postwar Detroit to have been a vibrant and extremely influential center in the development and continuation of bebop well into the 1950s. Additionally, her training in the church and her immersion in a family-centered system of musical mentorship provide both insight into the processes of musical transmission in black urban communities and an alternative to the stories of individual male genius that dominate jazz criticism.

In a similar fashion, Alice Coltrane's rapid development from a bebop pianist to an avant-garde player during the mid-1960s is best seen within a frame of interpenetrating spheres of influence. Alice's musical metamorphosis cannot be separated from her marriage to John Coltrane, from his mentorship, and from their spiritual explorations. Likewise, these explorations cannot be dissociated from the larger transformation of black cultural politics during the civil rights era. Moreover, viewing the couple's search for universal spirituality and their commitment to avant-garde jazz as a vehicle of transcendence directs attention away from the political rebellion of the period and toward its equally important counterpart, spiritual revolution. Exploring Alice's musical development, then, requires us to consider how countercultural spiritual explorations among black musicians influenced the aesthetics of avant-garde musical expression. Furthermore, while the study of ritual practices has figured prominently in both ethnomusicological studies of non-Western music and in musicological works devoted to Western art music from past centuries, it has been noticeably absent in studies of post-1960s jazz and contemporary experimental music.

Finally, Alice Coltrane's transformation from musician to guru offers an insight into her evolving compositional aesthetics and, in turn, reveals the exceptional fluidity of ritual practices in late modern Western society. Her impulse and ability to create a new musical and spiritual tradition speaks not only to her own vision and means, but also to a historical moment ripe for invention, reinvention, and new modes of self-realization. As Eric Hobsbawm has argued, "there is probably no time and place with which historians are not concerned which has not seen the invention of tradition . . . However, we should expect it to occur more frequently when a rapid transformation of society weakens or destroys the social patterns for which 'old' traditions had been designated, producing new ones to which they were not applicable, or when such old traditions and their institutional carriers and promulgators no longer prove sufficiently adaptable and flexible" (Hobsbawm 1983, 5).

Alice Coltrane provides a valuable example of African American women's consistent participation and presence in jazz and American music. Her life and music challenge time-honored aesthetic binaries: those of composer/improviser, the art/jazz world, black/white, East/West, and secular/sacred. But as much as this life history may offer new insights into jazz history; African American musical and social history; notions of tradition, ritual, and identity; and feminism, it also restores and celebrates the contributions of an original and influential American composer, an improviser, and, above all, a devotional musician.

Ultimately, Alice's mystical orientation as an artist produced extraordinarily original music. Yet it was also her compulsion to testify, a ritual rooted in the traditions of her childhood, that produced such a unique body of work. As James Cone writes, testifying, though at the center of communal experience, is also "unquestionably . . . and primarily an individual story" (Cone 1982, 1). As we will see, the musical testimonials that appear throughout her prolific recording career, in her life as a performer, and in her role as a musical swami reveal a rich earthly life full of opportunities for artistic and spiritual growth.

CHAPTER ONE

God's Child in the Motor City

I heard music that was just beyond anything I had heard before. I would hear country gospel. I would hear the down-home gospel. I would hear the kind of gospel you almost wouldn't need music with. It was flowing from the heart, from the soul. —Alice Coltrane

Long before her artistic collaborations with John Coltrane, Alice Coltrane (1937–2007), née Alice McLeod, had already acquired a wealth of musical experience and a deep understanding of the spiritual power of music. An African American keyboard prodigy, she had the great fortune of growing up in a musical family in Detroit during its postwar heyday, a period in which the city's black musical subcultures invented some of the most influential musical styles of the twentieth century.

During the 1950s, Detroit had a reputation, particularly among African American performers and audiences, as a city whose high standards and heartfelt appreciation for modern jazz was unrivaled. Detroit's black musical community supplied New York's clubs and record producers with a steady source of second-generation bebop artists: performers such as Betty Carter, Ron Carter, Paul Chambers, Tommy Flanagan, Barry Harris, Elvin and Thad Jones, Yusef Lateef, and Terry Pollard are only some of Detroit's more famous sons and daughters. The city was also a jazz mecca, where out-of-town musicians could find employment and develop their ideas in a rigorous yet uniquely supportive environment. It was within this rich milieu of skilled players and African American musical cognoscenti that Alice McLeod learned her craft as a jazz pianist. In fact, listeners acquainted only with her more avant-garde explorations may be surprised to learn of her superior abilities as bebop pianist, which are little known outside Detroit's musical circles.

Yet long before her arrival on Detroit's jazz scene, she had developed her musical ability playing piano and organ for her neighborhood Baptist church, as well as for other congregations throughout the city. This was the so-called golden age of gospel in America, and Detroit's black churches were producing some of the most important African American keyboardists and singers of the twentieth century—artists such as Aretha Franklin, Marvin Gaye, Mom and Pop Winans, Stevie Wonder, and other Motown stars, whose mainstream success transformed popular music (Boyer 1995).

The setting of Alice Coltrane's early life is best described as a vibrant intersection of the sacred and secular musical spheres of her family, her neighborhood, the black churches in which she played, and the social and professional associations that constituted Detroit's jazz scene during the 1950s. These close, overlapping networks sustained and influenced the young Alice McLeod, and they are part of the greater social, musical, and religious history of African-Americans in postwar Detroit.

The Arsenal of Democracy

The majority of Detroit's black migrants came from the Deep South, and, apart from the older bourgeoisie, the community was known to have a "down home" Southern feeling compared to communities in Philadelphia and New York, where black citizens came from the more populated and industrialized mid-Atlantic states.[1] Like many African Americans who had migrated to Detroit between the world wars, Alice's parents were both natives of Alabama. Her mother, Ann Johnston, grew up in Athens, a small, rural town; her father, Solon McLeod, was raised in the city of Birmingham. Although Alice was not sure, it is probable that Ann and Solon McLeod met in Detroit during the mid-1920s. Ann had traveled there from Huntington, West Virginia, where she had lived with her first husband, Harold Farrow—she divorced him but they remained on friendly terms—and their two children, Ernest and Margaret, who would become Alice's half-siblings. Solon arrived in Detroit after serving in the First World War, one of a number of black veterans in search of work.

Despite the influx of African Americans, when Ann Johnston and Solon McLeod arrived in Detroit, blacks were only a small percent of the urban population—4.1 percent compared to 81 percent in 2000.[2] During this interwar period, Detroit was still a multiethnic manufacturing town; it had been attracting European immigrants and white American migrant workers since the turn of the century.[3] Situated on the Detroit River, with access to the Great Lakes, the city was home to the automotive industry and the largest steel foundry in the world. In addition to companies such as Ford, Chrysler, General Motors, and Dodge, the city also contained chemical plants, oil refineries, and many other smaller manufacturing companies. By the late 1920s, Detroit was "a sprawling web of industrial train tracks" and "innumerable blue collar neighborhoods" of African American, Canadian, German, Hungarian, Irish, Italian, Jewish, Lebanese, Lithuanian, Mexican, Palestinian, Polish, and Scottish families (Sugrue 1996, 22). Solon McLeod drove a truck for one of the many companies that delivered industrial items to the city's factories. Ann McLeod did not work, except on rare occasions as a domestic when the family needed extra money. Usually she stayed at home raising her growing family, which included six children by the late 1930s: Ernest and Margaret Farrow, and Jack, Joanne, Alice, and Marylin McLeod.

Alice was born August 27, 1937, and her childhood spanned the war years, a period of particularly volatile race relations in the city of Detroit. Automotive manufacturing plants were converted to the production of weapons, and "almost overnight" Detroit became part of the American military-industrial complex, earning the city the nickname of "the arsenal of democracy" (Sugrue 1996, 19). War mobilization brought Detroit 500,000 migrants from diverse ethnic backgrounds between 1940 and 1943, and the black population doubled. Ironically, although unemployment was at an all-time low, discrimination was endemic in the city that was working tirelessly to preserve freedom abroad.[4] Racial tension grew to such a degree that *Life* magazine stated in a 1942 headline that "the city can either blow up Hitler or blow up the U.S." ("Detroit Is Dynamite," 15). With the return of black GIs after the war, formal protests against discrimination began. In April 1943, the NAACP and the UAW organized an equal-opportunity rally that attracted 10,000 people. In response to the promotion of three black employees later that month, 26,000 white workers walked out of the Packard plant. Later that summer, the Belle Isle Riot, one of the worst race riots in American history, claimed the lives of thirty-four citizens (twenty-five of them black), in three days looting and racially motivated attacks.

By 1950, when Alice was thirteen, 357,857 black Americans had made a home in what was then the greatest industrial center in the United States. In spite of chronic racial tension and episodic violence, the black community succeeded in maintaining a culturally and economically self-sufficient subculture in what were to become increasingly segregated neighborhoods.[5] Woodward Avenue divided Detroit's largest African American residential area into the struggling East Side and the more affluent West Side, and residents often identified themselves accordingly as either East Siders or West Siders.[6]

An East Sider, Alice lived first in an apartment at 644 Farnsworth Avenue. During her teenage years, her family moved into a spacious home closer to Wayne State University, on a more affluent block but still east of Woodward Avenue. The neighborhood's residents were predominantly poor and working-class families who lived in tenements and subdivided wood-frame houses. The jazz bassist Vishnu Wood (né William Clifford), a future collaborator who later introduced Alice to her guru, Swami Satchidananda, was a fellow East Sider at the time. He described the community as "Southern" and "rough and tumble" (interview with author, 2001). Gangs made their presence known in the streets, and young people developed both a street-smart edge and a tight network of friends and family who provided community support and a safety network under challenging circumstances. By contrast, the West Side demonstrated greater evidence of rising social mobility. More families owned their own homes, the public schools were of better quality, and young adults typically went on to college and other forms of professional training (Sugrue 1996, 36–40).

To some extent, these neighborhood demographics reflected the beginnings of the class stratification and class consciousness that developed in African American communities after the Second World War.[7] However, families of differing economic and social status lived in close proximity.[8] In these overcrowded and sometimes unforgiving circumstances, a unique cultural exchange occurred in the black community that often bypassed class distinction, and music was one of the transcendent mediums. One of the most powerful organizations that emerged in black neighborhoods with respect to both musical and cultural exchange during this period was the urban black church.

The Conservatory at Mt. Olive

Like many large, mainstream churches, the McLeods' neighborhood church, Mt. Olive Baptist, catered to a broad cross section of Detroit's African American population by consciously appealing to the diverse musical tastes of its congregants. The standard repertoire for such congregations during the 1940s included spirituals that date back to slavery,[9] Calvinist hymns of the eighteenth century,[10] American and African American evangelical hymns of the Second Great Awakening,[11] and the new gospel repertoire[12] that was gaining in popularity.

The McLeods' church could boast several choirs. This configuration was relatively common: in larger Baptist and even Methodist congregations, two choirs were customarily used to satisfy the musical tastes of their members, with a senior choir singing hymns and anthems from the European American tradition, and a gospel choir singing in the newer urban style that was common in Holiness, Pentecostal, and Church of God in Christ establishments. Alice's mother, Ann McLeod, was fond of religious singing. She was a member of the Senior Choir of Mt. Olive Baptist, played piano, and possessed "a very natural ability for music and a beautiful alto voice" (A.

Coltrane, interview with author, 2001). Ann's first husband was the choir director at Mt. Olive Baptist. He had a reputation for "great musical knowledge" and "excellence" as a keyboardist and musical director (ibid.).

Although she began taking private piano lessons at the age of seven, Alice described Mt. Olive Baptist as the primary locus of her early musical education. Moved by her older half-brother Ernest Farrow's commitment to musical study (he became one of Detroit's finest jazz bassists), she became possessed by a desire to play the piano, even though there was none in her home. Although an extremely shy child, she mustered the courage to ask her neighbor Mrs. Philpot for lessons. Alice explained, "I was hesitant to say that I would like for her to teach me. But I approached her, and she obliged, and it was great, starting out with little scales and simplistic solos" (ibid.). Her weekly lessons lasted two years, at which point Mrs. Philpot requested that Alice "continue and seek higher training with either her teacher or possibly at a music school" (ibid.).

During this period, Alice had demonstrated her talents playing simple solos for Sunday school, and it quickly became apparent to her congregation that she was a precocious musician. In a gesture typical of the social engagement of black mainstream churches, Mt. Olive's congregation offered to sponsor Alice for a year of study at the community music school in her neighborhood. With good instruction and accessible facilities, the school fostered her rapid development. In fact, after her year there, she did not study again music formally until her teenage years—she acquired her skills on the job, as a church pianist.

Alice considered her musical education at Mt. Olive Baptist to be "a gradation or graduation of sorts." There she learned to play piano and organ for Mt. Olive's three large choirs: the Young People's Choir, the Senior Choir, and the Pastor's Choir. Although Alice was musically literate and often used church hymnals, her training is best viewed as in the oral, or aural, tradition. Church hymnals provide the keyboardist with only a melodic and harmonic skeleton, similar to a jazz lead sheet. The ornamental, rhythmic, improvisatory, and timbral characteristics of black church music—qualities that clearly distinguish it from music in white Protestant churches—are part of an aurally transmitted black musical aesthetic. For instance, when I asked if anybody had taught her how to play for her church, Alice stated, "Nobody really, but you had some musical guidelines. But the rhythmical aspect, that came from the experience . . . I really think most of it just comes from the environment" (ibid.).

According to Alice, learning to play for the different choirs was a hands-on learning experience that required different stylistic skills on her part. She explained:

For the young people, there were all the written musical pieces that I would play for them to sing. There wasn't as much rhythmical involvement there. Senior Choir was very nice, sort of strict, leaning toward the European anthems; a number of them were beautiful hymns from the hymn book. There was not a great deal of additional work needed other than being able to read . . . but when you are playing in the Pastor's chorus, you have to play in a different kind of way. The Pastor's chorus sounds like gospel. You have the gospel songs, from a book called *Gospel Pearls,* if you can find it. Beautiful songs. (ibid.)

Gospel Pearls (1921) was one of the most popular hymnals of the time.[13] It included simple reductions of Protestant and gospel hymns by white writers, as well as Negro spirituals and newly composed black gospel songs.[14] According to Horace Boyer, the publication of *Gospel Pearls* was a clear indication that gospel music had "crossed denominational music boundaries . . . Baptists no longer had to attend Pentecostal, Holiness, or Sanctified churches to hear the music. They could now hear this music in their own churches on Sunday mornings" (1995, 44). Although gospel repertoire had become standard fare, different denominations in Northern cities performed the music in their own preferred fashion. Boyer distinguishes two overarching styles of singing gospel: "one that emphasized singing in which the spirit dictated the amount of embellishment, volume and improvisation that was applied, and a second that, while attempting to incorporate the dictates of the spirit, tempered the rendition to the musical taste of the Baptist Congregation" (ibid.). Although gospel music at Mt. Olive was of this second variety, music was of no less importance to the congregation.

As a budding church pianist and organist, Alice had numerous responsibilities. In the Baptist service, each liturgical event is typically set off by a musical offering, so that the sonic component often constitutes at least half the time allotted to the church service. The pianist typically interacts with the pastor in the form of punctuating or dramatizing the sermon. The pianist also brings the congregation together in hymn singing. In the gospel portion of the service, music is expected to lead to a particularly high level of emotional intensity and expressive release for the congregation. Elements of musical performance such as dramatic shifts in timbre and register, highly syncopated rhythm, and flexible improvisational structures are tailored to the emotional peaks of the ritual and support this purpose of spiritual transformation.

In retrospect, one can see how these musical skills came to serve Alice in a variety of improvisational contexts outside the church. In a very practical sense, her church training provided her with many of the requisite skills for life as a professional jazz musician: she was required to sight read, arrange spontaneously from a lead sheet, and listen and respond intently to a soloist or the pastor. She was also required to improvise musical statements and continually adapt her aesthetics, depending on the communal energy of the moment. Playing for services and weekly rehearsals was on-the-job training.

Even more important, playing in church gave Alice the opportunity to gain musical confidence and exercise a degree of artistic power that might not have been available to her in the male-dominated secular realm. Traditionally, the church has been an acceptable performance space for African American women, where for generations they have flourished as keyboardists and singers. As church musicians, women have been the unrecognized teachers of many reputable jazz stylists. For instance, female church pianists were the first musical influences on the jazz progenitors Eubie Blake and Fats Waller (Unterbrink 1983, 40). Other women also developed musical techniques that became standard fare in both the sacred and secular realms: the keyboardists Arizona Dranes and Sallie Sanders were largely responsible for the evolution of the pentecostal playing style, which later became common in up-tempo rhythm-and-blues numbers. Alice was part of this time-honored yet undervalued tradition of female church pianists.

"God-Inspired"

As Alice developed her skills, she was invited to play in other churches in Detroit where musical services were particularly ecstatic. She credited the Lemon Gospel Choir at the Mack Avenue Church of God in Christ for the most powerful musical and religious experiences of her youth. The Lemon Gospel Choir was the musical home of Deloris Ranson, the choir pianist, and David Winans. They would become the future matriarch and patriarch of Detroit's most famous family of gospel singers. "Mom and Pop" Winans, as they are known in the gospel industry, gave birth to ten children—two of whom, Cece and Bebe, have won Grammy awards.

Independent Holiness sects such as the Mack Avenue Church of God were and are particularly known for their musical and expressive ties to African American folk churches and the religious culture of slave society. As these small, independent congregations came North, the lively musical practices of the invisible church were maintained, with hand clapping, foot stomping, and call-and-response forms. As these "folk churches" or "shouting churches"[15] grew in popularity, they generated a rise in what the black community called "old-time religion." By the 1920s, the highly interactive musical style of many of these independent sects had developed into a distinctive genre, displaying particularly ecstatic versions of European American sacred hymnody, Negro spirituals, and urban blues and jazz.[16]

Alice said that playing for the Lemon Gospel Choir "was the gospel experience . . . of [her] life." It gave her a profound understanding of "down home" religion and the spiritual power of music for African Americans, as well as the experience of unmediated worship at the collective level, which she would replicate in her life as a devotional musician. Similar to possession ceremonies found throughout West Africa, at the Mack Avenue Church of God in Christ, congregants would become "highly overcome" and require tending. Alice's account demonstrates an unusually positive attitude toward the sanctified service—many Baptist churchgoers would be put off by such emotional abandon and seeming disorder—and a moment in Detroit when the postwar gospel tradition was in full flower:

> There was another choir that my parents permitted me to be involved in when I was a little older. I must have been around fifteen or sixteen. A chorus called the Lemon Gospel Singers. Now that was the gospel experience, musically, of my life! Because not only were they singing! Some of the time, when we were invited to other churches, I mean, I heard music that was just beyond anything I had heard before. I would hear country gospel. I would hear the down-home gospel. I would hear the kind of gospel you almost wouldn't need music with. It was flowing from the heart, from the soul. After a while there was no music.
>
> One day we were at this church. I was with the young people, ages fifteen to nineteen. I happened not to be at the piano at the time because there were two of us, and the other pianist could play anything—she was superb. The choir was singing and there was such a spiritual experience happening in that church. There was such God feeling. The people in the audience were so overcome with the spirit, they weren't singing anymore; some were just walking around the church. Half of the choir had to be carried out—even young people. The Lord just completely swept through. The pianist started playing at such a rapid pace, and everything just stopped. What could you do? All you could do was go and sit down. There were no closing remarks, there was no more singing, there were nurses attending to those who were highly overcome, and some were carried downstairs, and that was it. The service was never dismissed by the minister. Just God. God-inspired. An experience filled with the spirit of the Lord. (A. Coltrane, interview with author, 2001)

Alice McLeod's early experiences playing for Baptist and Independent denominations in Detroit influenced her aesthetic sensibilities and inspired a lifelong passion for ecstatic and collective forms of musical expression. Her musical experiences were marked by an ethos of flexibility and eclecticism in which music served the multifaceted purposes of religious expression, communal participation, and cultural and historical validation. More important, the most inspirational musical activities in church for her were free of fixed form and structure, and were always inspired by an unmediated relationship with the Lord. While she replicated aspects of this gospel worship style at Sai Anantam Ashram in her *bhajan* arrangements, as we will see, she also maintained many of these aesthetics throughout her professional career—on the bandstand with her husband, in her own jazz ensembles, and even playing bebop as a young woman.

Beyond Mt. Olive

Although the church was the primary locus of Alice's early musical experiences, her creative, artistic, and intellectual aspirations broadened during her adolescence. She continued to work as a professional church pianist, but she also began to apply her precocious keyboard skills to the mastery of classical music and modern jazz. For a variety of reasons, classical music was not a viable professional career for most African Americans at the time, particularly for those from the East Side of Detroit. Preprofessional training requires hours of study as a young child, with master teachers who possess the proper pedigree or lineage. Alice's socioeconomic status, coupled with widespread institutional racism barring blacks from professional classical music institutions, would almost certainly have stood in the way had she wanted to pursue this path.[17] Alice, however, never said that classical music performance was her primary ambition. While she taught herself a great deal of the canonical classical piano repertoire over the years, she studied it only intermittently as a teen. Classical music, nonetheless, did remain an important part of her life:

> I did have another private teacher for a short time, but her name is gone from my memory. She was an aged lady, but very nice. I probably studied about six months with her. But what I really carried forward was the importance of really keeping your music alive—even the classical music alive. Just take all the books, practice, keep your reading up to par. It's important to me. And from time to time I do it. I still put up the classical music. It brings the path to now. I'm kind of sorry there is no more beautiful music coming from Europe, and Russia, and places like that. Back in those days in the 1800s there was more incentive or motivation to write beautiful classical themes or symphonic themes and present them. Now it's still Stravinsky, Rimsky-Korsakov, Bach, Beethoven, Mendelssohn, It's still those people that get played. Grieg and Mozart. (ibid.)

Fortunately, Alice McLeod's African American musical subculture gave her numerous opportunities to grow as an artist. Her teenage years spanned what the Detroit jazz historian Lars Bjorn and his colleague Jim Gallert (2001) have called the city's golden age, a period in which "the economy was booming and a take-care-of-business ethos flourished amidst a peer group of young aspirants" (Panken 2000, 44). During the 1950s, Detroit's industrial economy provided an economic base for a thriving entertainment business; the levels of jazz musicianship and audience expectation in the city were extremely high. As the baritone saxophonist Pepper Adams explained, "You see, in Detroit the standards were so high, to compete for local gigs you had to play awful goddam good. If you were good enough to be competitive in Detroit, you were far ahead of what the rest of the world's standards were" (quoted in Carner 1990, 21). Detroit's standards were such that Alice's musical role models—African American pianists active on the scene during her youth—included Tommy Flanagan, Barry Harris, Terry Pollard, and Roland Hannah, some of the finest players in the modern jazz tradition.

Several historical factors contributed to the exceptional quality of black musicianship in Detroit during the 1950s. Crucial determinants included the continuity of Detroit's jazz tradition and the many venues in the city that had supported black instrumental music since its emergence in the first decades of the twentieth century. Like cosmopolitan centers such as Chicago and New York, Detroit was a magnet for musicians who had the requisite skills to play for society dance bands in the city's numerous ballrooms.[18] Although audiences were segregated, black bands played for both whites and blacks.[19] When ballroom entertainment declined during the Great Depression, so-called black-and-tan clubs similar to those in Harlem began to proliferate in Detroit's East Side. Paradise Valley, as it was called, in the heart of the city's largest black neighborhood, emerged as the center of nightlife during the 1930s and 1940s. Large floor shows featuring jazz orchestras were common at venues such as the Plantation and the Chocolate Bar.[20]

During this era of Ellington-style floor shows and swing bands, a jazz subculture developed in after-hours sessions and lasted well into the 1960s. The creative environment of Detroit's after-hours sessions during the late 1930s and 1940s was similar to those now-legendary jams sessions at Minton's Play House in New York that fostered many of the bebop innovations. Stylists such as Dizzy Gillespie, Charlie Parker, and Bud Powell, artists responsible for the modernist approach, were either New York natives or musicians who had already achieved national success before coming to New York.[21] By contrast, Detroit jazz sessions were homegrown, local affairs. The city could not boast of a jazz recording industry, nor could its jazz musicians expect national recognition or international success. For the most part, Detroit's jazz players, particularly during the 1950s, were born or grew up there.

Although influenced by national musical trends, particularly bebop, players incorporated these innovations to fit the tastes of local audiences, and a distinct brand of modern jazz emerged in the city, one that required musicians to be fluent in multiple genres, know a huge repertoire, and always respect the entertainment value of the music. When the bebop style caught the attention of Detroit's young musical modernists, the new language was often played alongside rhythm-and-blues selections that were extremely popular among black audiences during the era.[22] Barry Harris, whom Alice described as "a musician of the highest order," was the central figure of a group of young, mostly black, musical intellectuals exploring the music of Charlie Parker, Bud Powell, and their associates during the early 1950s (A. Coltrane, interview with author, 2001). Harris described how audience members danced to up-tempo bebop standards such as "Cherokee":

> At that time you had to know a certain amount of tunes: rhythm-and-blues was powerful then, you had to play shuffle rhythm all night long and some of the really famous standards . . . You see, the jazz musicians came in playing their songs, they played their music. Bird played fast. There used to be a shake dancer named Baby Scruggs and she would shake dance to "Cherokee" as fast as you could play it. You had to see that. It would knock you out! Boy she was fine, you had to dig it! It was like a whole thing. We danced to "Cherokee," we danced fast tunes and slow tunes, it didn't have to be a slow tune you knew to dance. Jazz musicians made their own blues and stuff so you danced their blues like you danced anybody else's blues. People danced and they knew the songs, they knew if you messed up, or if the drummer turned the beat around. Our contemporaries were there while we were playing what we wanted to play. Man, it was beautiful. (Harris 1995, 17)

In addition to integrating the dance-based nightlife, Detroit's highly supportive, yet critical black audiences were also an important contributing factor to the exceptional quality of Detroit jazz. According to the world-renowned bassist Cecil McBee, who spent several years "getting it together in Detroit" before going on to New York (and whom Alice employed in the late 1960s as a sideman), the black audiences, whom he described as "the intellectuals," demanded that a player "reach deep inside":

> They had to hear that—from the deepest part of your stomach. You knew if you were successful by the response of the audience and you knew and you were relieved because you knew that you had connected. And you would play yourself to death until the wee hours of the morning. Here was a place that you could express or experiment on whatever you were working on, and the crowd knew that that was the deal. They knew that the goal was to experiment individually and collectively and to reach out to the stars so far as your development was concerned. (McBee, interview with author, 2001)

The postwar economy in Detroit also contributed to what McBee described as Detroit's intellectual jazz culture. The city's public secondary schools, such as Cass Technical and Miller High School, had exceptional music programs. Cass required high academic standing and an audition to specialize in music there. Essentially a classical music conservatory, Cass trained such Detroit jazz artists as Billy Mitchell, Tommy Flannagan, Ron Carter, and Paul Chambers. Chambers described the program:

The curriculum took up a whole day of music. That's why it took a couple more years to graduate. For example, we'd have the first period chamber music, the second period full orchestra, third either harmony or counterpoint and rudiments, then came piano and the academic classes . . . I used to get together with Doug Watkins, Donald Byrd, and piano player Hugh Lawson in rest periods, and we'd play. (Chambers 1961, 15)

Miller High was renowned for the music pedagogue Milton Cabrera, whose insistence on harmonic knowledge and classical technique and whose touring high-school big band trained the likes of Milt Jackson, Yusef Lateef, and the Burrell brothers. Such exceptional public high schools gave Detroit's musical youth a huge advantage, providing them with virtuoso skills and a full understanding of functional harmony. Young African American musicians brought an extremely broad musical knowledge to the many forms of popular music that were professionally available. This gave Detroit a unique reputation as a place where young jazz players "really knew their chords."[23]

Garfield Middle School and North Eastern High School, which Alice attended, did not possess the strongest music programs in the city. The fact that her secondary-school education had little influence on her musical development testifies to her own single-mindedness as an aspiring musician, as well as the strength of the other musical networks to which she belonged. She did, however, play percussion in North Eastern's concert band, an unusual choice for a young woman at the time. The reed player Bennie Maupin—who later got his big musical break playing on Herbie Hancock's *Headhunters* LP—went to the same high school and was Alice's close friend and colleague for many years. He recalled:

She was playing timpani and chimes and glockenspiel and snare drum and all the percussion stuff that's found in an orchestra or symphonic band, and I was just really impressed with that, because you don't think of women or young ladies doing that. But she was there. And it was quite obvious that she really had a very good grasp of what she was doing. It was interesting to watch her going from one instrument to the other and to hear what she was actually doing with those instruments. (Maupin, telephone interview with author, 2001)

Maupin, several years her junior, also remembered that Alice was already an accomplished jazz pianist by her high-school years:

I came into the auditorium with my class, and we sat down and I looked up on the stage, and there was Alice playing the piano! And I didn't know she played the piano, but she was playing the piano. And then she actually had a trio, she had a drummer and she had a bass player, and then I found out later that she had actually been teaching them how to accompany her. She was always teaching, always very far ahead, you know? I was just very impressed by her abilities and what she could do, and when I heard her play the piano I was just so in awe of her because I hadn't heard anyone play like that . . . Well she was playing some tune, I didn't know what tune it was because I didn't know that many songs, but I knew that she was improvising on whatever it was. And they played it and the kids went wild after it was over. (ibid.)

Motown's Modern Jazz Network

One might imagine that the perilous, sin-filled "conservatory of the streets" that has stereotypically constituted the bebop musician's training ground would have been off-limits to a young, church-going woman from a respectable family.[24] Yet several facets of Detroit's jazz scene gave Alice the critical musical access and professional exposure she needed to fully develop her skills and reputation as an accomplished bebop musician by her early twenties. The Detroit modern jazz network during the 1950s was a bourgeois operation in comparison to jazz networks in other urban centers.[25] It was small, close-knit, and dominated by several important jazz family dynasties, including the Burrells (brothers Billy and Kenny), the Jacksons (brothers Milton, Alvin, and Oliver), the Jones family (brothers Hank, Thad, and Elvin), and the McKinneys (brothers Harold, Ray, and William).[26]

The high percentage of black homeownership in Detroit during the 1940s and 1950s, even among working-class people, contributed to the strength of family jazz networks, as well as to the overall quality of black music.[27] Living in a house rather than a tenement was conducive to the musical mastery needed for bebop. Space to practice and jam with peers without fear of bothering the neighbors, as well as the support of a financially stable family, was a great benefit to many young black musicians coming of age. Sessions in the Jones, McKinney, and Harris homes, for instance, were common (Bjorn and Gallert 2001, 130).

Barry Harris would regularly gather the finest Detroit musicians in his family home to work on new concepts: "My mother was beautiful to all of us, Donald Byrd, Paul (Cambers) and Doug (Watkins). My house was a classroom. We could practice all we wanted" (quoted in Bourne 1985, 27). Harris explained:

In Manhattan it's mostly apartment buildings, and you can't play an instrument in an apartment building. Learning an instrument would be impossible. You had people from places like Brooklyn or the Bronx who owned separate homes, and they could do whatever they wanted there. Places like my place, we lived in a two-family building. Sometimes the people downstairs had a party and we would go and play, we jammed all the time. There really was a musical environment. (Harris 1995, 16)

Harris further likened this domestic environment to late-nineteenth-century salon society:

> In my house we would play all day long, not for anybody; we would play and try to learn . . . Donald Byrd was there, and Paul Chambers, the Jones Brothers, young musicians. We had more what the musical greats had years ago: they had salons, that's where Chopin, Liszt, all of them would gather, play, share information and learn from each other. (ibid.)

Although Alice's home was not a central hub in this "salon society," it was a meeting place for a great deal of Detroit talent. Most of the members of Alice's immediate family were either directly or indirectly involved in music: her mother sang in church, her older brother, Jackie McLeod, was a stylishly dressed fixture in Detroit's jazz clubs. Alice's younger sister, Marilyn, a year and a half her junior, would go on to write successful commercial music for Motown Records. As Alice explained, "she was never interested in performance, but she has written a lot of music and some well-known pieces. She had a song for Diana Ross called 'Love Hangover.' She got gold on that. And another one, 'Walk in the Night,' that was always playing" (interview with author, 2001).

By far the most crucial to Alice's development as a young jazz musician—aside from her own innate talents—was the presence and influence of her older half-brother, Ernest Farrow, who, during Alice's formative years, was fast becoming one of Detroit's finest modern jazz musicians. Alice credited Ernest for much of her early jazz education:

> My brother, who is not living, played bass. That meant I got to hear everything that he was doing. And when allowed, I would go with him to the sessions and hear what the musicians were playing. And I really believed I could learn what I heard. I said, "I believe I can play this music if I put my mind to it." He showed me as much as he could . . . I feel that he was a big inspiration for me. Had he not been in the house, I don't know. (ibid.)

Nine years her senior, Ernest played alto saxophone in North Eastern's concert band, as well as in ensembles for local parties, dances, and amateur contests. Alice recalls that she was always hearing recordings of "the latest thing" that inspired her brother during the 1940s, particularly "Sarah Vaughan, Lester Young, and Charlie Parker" (ibid.). By the time Alice was studying piano and playing at church, Ernest had switched to the acoustic bass, the instrument on which he would make a lasting contribution during his tragically abbreviated career as a professional musician. (Ernest Farrow died in a drowning accident in 1969—a great tragedy for his family and the jazz community, and one of many personal losses that Alice would endure.)

Barry Harris, whom Ernest had befriended in his youth, recalled the day Ernest switched from saxophone to acoustic bass. "Ernie was the cat I really grew up with all the way . . . Ernie started out as an alto player. We were going to play an amateur show at the Paradise Theatre, and he didn't play alto as good as James Thompson, so he played the bass. That's how he started on the bass. All he did was say, 'I'll play the bass,' and he played it."[28] Although Ernest's abilities rivaled those of many bass players who later became famous after leaving Detroit, he chose to stay in the city to raise his family. Cecil McBee, who spent several years in the early 1960s developing his own bass playing in Detroit before going to New York, described Ernest as "one of the first people that was very advanced on the instrument":

> He was far more advanced than the Ron Carters and Paul Chambers because he had a triple finger technique. This was rather novel at the time. You know I thought I was introducing it at the time but I ran into him and he had been working on it long before I was. He was really a great bass player . . . You know I thought he would have fared better if he had spent the time working on it rather than dealing with his family and other more socially involved things contrary to the music. Had he really stepped out there and made music everything he probably would have been one of the world's greatest bass players. (McBee, interview with author, 2001)

Bennie Maupin described Ernest Farrow's lasting impact on the next generation of bass players:

> Ernie was just awesome. I mean, he was so incredible . . . There are a couple of bass players who really stand out from Detroit. The one of course is Paul Chambers, who when he was fifteen or sixteen was playing with Miles Davis. Then there was another named Doug Watkins—died in an automobile accident when he was very young. They were very much touched by Ernie because Ernie was a bit older than them . . . his sound, his time, the language that he used . . . It was really a sad thing [his passing], because he was such a great talent and the warmest personality. (Maupin, telephone interview with author, 2001)

Alice was also extremely fortunate to have had the guidance of Ernest's musical associates, in particular Barry Harris, called the "high priest of bebop," who has since been responsible for teaching scores of jazz musicians the harmonic, rhythmic, and melodic language of modern jazz. As Ernest's close friend and musical partner, and the long-time suitor of Alice's older half-sister, Margaret, Harris was a regular visitor at the McLeods'. Alice explained:

> The family thought Barry was going to marry my sister. He took her to the prom. We thought they were the king and queen of Detroit. Barry was like my own brother . . . He has shown me so much, chords, and voicings. He was at the house often,

and they would all go out and he would play professionally with my brother. (A. Coltrane, interview with author, 2001)

Other influential jazz pianists also frequented the McLeod home and would show Alice various techniques. Terry Pollard, another famous female pianist from Detroit, became an important mentor to the young Alice McLeod. Ms. Pollard, a musical colleague and love interest of Ernest's for many years, gave the McLeods their first piano, "an old upright," when Alice was just a girl.[29] Later, when Alice was a young woman, Terry Pollard recommended her to bandleaders, local club owners, and promoters.

On the Scene

By the time Alice was an aspiring jazz musician, Ernest had solidly established himself within Detroit's professional community, playing steady engagements in sought-after West Side venues such as the Bohemian Club, Klein's Show Bar, and the Blue Bird Inn, for the most accomplished composers and arrangers in the city.[30] At Klein's, Ernest played for the bandleader Hindal Butts in a band that included the pianist Hugh Lawson, the trombonist Curtis Fuller, and the saxophonist Pepper Adams, all of whom left for New York shortly thereafter to earn international recognition. At the Blue Bird, Ernest played in the house band under the leader Yusef Lateef, with the trumpeter Donald Byrd, the drummer Frank Gant, and the euphonium player Bernard McKinney (later Kiane Zawadi).

In 1958, at the Blue Bird, Ernest led his own band, the International Jazz Quartet, composed of the altoist Sonny Red, the pianist Hugh Lawson, and the drummer Oliver Jackson, and Joe Henderson while he was attending Wayne State University. Ernest's tenure as the leader at the Blue Bird was "a banner year" for the club (Bjorn and Gallert 2001, 117). It had recently reopened after renovations and featured big names such as Miles Davis and his sextet, as well as the bands of Horace Silver, Art Blakey, and Jimmy Smith. Former Detroiters Sonny Stitt, Billy Mitchell, Thad Jones, and Milt Jackson also returned in 1958 to play engagements at the club.

Ernest often took Alice to jam sessions during this period, exposing her to the many formidable musicians who were his colleagues. As she put it:

I think my environment was the sessions—when you would sit in at a session, you would make your friends, and once you were known you were called for jobs. You had to make yourself known. People would say there's a session here or there. You know once John Coltrane came to town and they called me and I don't know, I wasn't available. You know people would say you missed it! Trane was here. You should have heard it! Every time he played over a G minor 7, and then—it was like that! All the musicians would flock. Whoever was in town—Miles Davis came into town. (A. Coltrane, interview with author, 2001)

Kenneth Cox recalled hearing her regularly at the West End Hotel's after-hours session, and at the home of Joe Brazil in Conant Gardens. Jam sessions at Joe Brazil's were highly regarded among jazz musicians, and talent passing through the city would frequently show up to play. While on tour in Detroit, John Coltrane did indeed attend sessions, and, according to Cox, it was at Joe Brazil's that Alice first met her future husband, although she recounted that their formal introduction occurred in New York several years later.

Alice's first working band in Detroit was a group called the Premieres—"a lounge act," to use the bassist Vishnu Wood's description of the band—that fused the quartet singing of gospel and rhythm-and-blues genres with jazz improvisation. The members of the Premiers (George Bohanon, trombone; Anthony Jackson, bass; Oliver Jackson, drums; and Alice, organ) were each accomplished instrumentalists and strong singers. The group found steady work in local show bars as well as in the resort areas outside the city. Acts such as the Premiers were common in Detroit, providing a model for many of the talented musical acts that Berry Gordy Jr. later made famous at Motown records. The Premieres were particularly busy in 1956. Their engagements at the Eagle Show Bar and La Vert's Lounge and Bowl, two popular Detroit venues, were regularly advertised in the *Michigan Chronicle*. They were also regularly booked at the Eagle Show Bar in 1958.

Between 1956 and 1960, while playing for the Premiers, Alice also performed in various engagements when groups needed a pianist: she recalls having accompanied both Yusef Lateef and Sonny Stitt in the late 1950s. While developing her professional musical career during this period after high school, Alice met her first husband, Kenneth Hagood, a native of Detroit. Eleven years her senior, "Poncho" Hagood was by then a reputable bebop scat singer who had recorded with Thelonious Monk, Dizzy Gillespie, Charlie Parker, and Miles Davis. Famous for his vocals on the bebop classic "Oop-Bop-A-Da," Hagood had returned to Detroit to find employment during the late 1950s and was playing local gigs with Ernest when Alice emerged on the scene.

In 1960, the young couple decided they would travel to Paris together and find work. This was a choice that many notable jazz musicians had made since the 1920s. However, by the early 1960s, living abroad had become particularly appealing. Jazz had generally lost its commercial appeal, replaced by rhythm and blues and its white cousin, rock and roll. Finding work, particularly as a bebop-oriented musician, had become increasingly difficult as musicians playing divergent jazz styles (modal jazz, hard-bop, cool, third stream, and the much contested avant-garde experimentation of Ornette Coleman and his sidemen) were all competing for limited resources and venues. A circle of bebop musicians was thriving abroad, and Poncho and Alice felt that they would do well in Europe. On the recommendation of her family, who did not deem it proper or safe for Alice to travel to Paris with Hagood out of wedlock, the two were married.

Alice spent nearly a year in Paris, where she was struck, as many African American artists have been, by the way the city was "culturally minded, culturally oriented, so appreciative of American music" (ibid.). She worked steadily amid a community of exiled musicians such as Lucky Thompson, Oscar Pettiford, Kenny Clarke, and Hazel Scott, and she recalled playing in upscale jazz venues that drew an international jet-setting crowd, including Prince Ali Kahn, Rita Hayworth, and Elvis and Priscilla Presley.

In Paris, Alice met her musical mentor Bud Powell and spent a good deal of time with his family at their home. Powell was "a guiding light" for Alice: "His sound, his knowledge of chord changes, dexterity. I felt that he was the best inspiration for me—well I can't say the best, John Coltrane was the best—but he was a great inspiration" (ibid.). Her time with the Powells gave her an opportunity to sit by the great pianist whose lengthy melodic constructions and bebop figures she would closely emulate, particularly in her recorded work with Terry Gibbs. The Powell residence was also a place of familial and spiritual sustenance for her:

> Sometimes we would have, what would you call it . . . at home reunions. We would sit down and talk about Detroit and New York. Talk about the family. Talk about the children, the music. Talk about church! We would do that and they were very heartfelt times. We would reminisce about roots, family, and friends. Those who were not with you now, and some only God knows when or if you would see them again. So those were very special moments. Almost like sacred moments. Sometimes we would even sing a hymn or two, or a gospel song. It was just beautiful . . . I have always stayed close to the church, wherever I was. (ibid.)

I find it characteristic that during her busy professional life, she still sought the company of family and spiritually minded individuals with whom she could "raise a hymn." The following year, while living in New York, she attended church every Sunday in Harlem with her mother's sister, Margaret Johnston. This spiritual orientation was present, in various forms, throughout her professional career.

Although her time in Paris was musically and culturally enriching, it was also a period of hardship, which may account for her needing to seek the support of the Powell family. In Paris, Alice became pregnant with her first child, Michelle; concurrently, her marriage with Hagood began to deteriorate. Although Alice was reluctant to discuss the matter, several of her Detroit colleagues have insinuated that Hagood struggled with drug addiction at the time. Michelle was born in Paris in 1960. By the time Alice and Michelle returned to the States, Poncho and Alice were legally divorced.

Although Alice never spoke publicly of the period as one of difficulty, life as a single mother and a freelance musician at the age of twenty-three must have been an extraordinary challenge. The professional compromises that she was forced to make were considerable. On her return from Paris, she had wanted to move to New York to pursue a formal musical education. This dream, however, was superseded by the practical decision to get a day job in Manhattan. She explained:

> I wanted to just go study. I wanted to go back to the books, to some technical basics. I thought if I studied for a year that would be sufficient. Then I could continue with what I was doing. But it didn't turn out that way. After a family discussion, it came up that I should work instead and I agreed that I should work and not go [to school]. I had applied to Juilliard and also applied at the Manhattan School. But, after that discussion, she, Auntie [Margaret Johnston], thought it better that I work, not being able to foresee what might be forthcoming. So I went to work as a file clerk. But it wasn't long after that, maybe two or three months, my brother showed up and I just started working full time [as a musician]. (ibid.)

Ernest frequently came to New York to work, and he recommended his sister for various jobs, as did Barry Harris, who was by then living in the city as well. Alice played regularly with the tenor saxophonist Johnny Griffin and remembers the numerous musicians from Detroit who were quite successful in the city at the time. She soon realized that she could make more money by playing music than by working a day job. However, it was difficult raising her daughter at such a distance from her extended family. After nearly a year in New York, she decided to return to Detroit and pursue her music there, a choice that Ernest had also made.

When Alice returned to Detroit, she and Michelle moved in with her parents. Between late 1960 and early 1962, Alice found steady work playing as a solo artist or with a bassist in various show bars. One in particular, the Hobby Bar, a reputable piano bar on Linwood Avenue, showcased local talent and was often a meeting place for local musicians. Alice also became the leader of a sextet that worked regularly in the city and its environs. This was a modern jazz ensemble consisting of valve trombonist George Bohanon from the Premieres, Frank Morelli and Bennie Maupin on reeds, George Goldsmith on drums, and Melvin Jackson on the bass. Alice wrote the arrangements, which consisted of work by contemporary jazz composers as well as her compositions.

During this period, her friendship with Bennie Maupin blossomed, and the two spent a great deal of time exploring various musical ideas. At her family home, with Michelle crawling on the floor, the two worked on pieces for the ensemble. Maupin described her as a great mentor:

> Alice and I would be in the living room listening to whatever we were listening to, or she's playing something for me on the piano, or helping me to interpret some of her stuff, you know, working on a lot of different things with her. In retrospect, I realize I was working on my ear training. She was teaching me things about, you know, voice leading—she was teaching me about how to interpret her music, specifically. And about phrasing and about all kinds of different stuff. You don't think about it when you're young like that, you're just kind of grabbing ahold of it. That was a period that was maybe a two-year period or something like that, but you know all of that I consider very significant. And I don't think that she realizes to this day how much she taught me. (Maupin, interview with author, 2001)

Maupin recalled Alice's remarkable ability to transcribe almost anything she heard from a record and immediately put it on paper for the band. One of the first projects he remembered her working on was a series of Thelonious Monk compositions that Hall Overton had arranged for a concert at Town Hall, in New York. Alice took the arrangement for a large ensemble and voiced it for the sextet, filling in harmonies on the piano where instrumental voices were absent.

Maupin also recalled that he and Alice would spend time listening to the music of other composers and improvisers. They were particularly fascinated with John Coltrane's recording *Africa Brass* (1961), which had recently been released. In fact, long before her personal and professional association with him, Alice's compositions for the sextet were influenced by the modal conception of John Coltrane and his contemporaries. Her original work tended to reach beyond the bebop genre for which Detroit was known. Though there are no recordings of the ensemble to explore, Maupin recalled Alice's compositional and improvisational technique as highly adventurous:

> Well you know, we had these forms that she had created. And so they would be, like, basically points of departure, but the improvisation that took place inside them was very adventurous. It wasn't like the standard, the AABA kind of tune like most bebop forms, or a twelve-bar blues, or something like that. I mean, we might have some of those too, but some of the forms were sort of extended, and the structures, just harmonically, were quite different. So, you know, there might be things that you couldn't quite put your ear on right away. And we were experimenting with the use of, you know, dissonances and, you know, just trying different scales and experimenting. I mean, we did a lot of that. And when people hear things that they

don't, that they aren't familiar with, some people gravitate towards it, some people shy away from it because it makes them uncomfortable, you know. And she was just like, man, I mean, sometimes I would just be standing there on the bandstand listening to how she was approaching these pieces.

You know, when you play with people sometimes you sort of get to know how they function? Some people play it safe. They'll play things pretty much the same each time. Alice never did. I mean, when she played, the lines would be uniquely different. And I listened to her enough to know they were different. I knew the lines were different, and it wasn't, she didn't repeat herself just because she knew the particular figure would work in a particular place or something. It was never about that—she was always reaching for something, you know? And that was just so very exciting, and impressed me to the extent that I'm very much that way, you know, myself. I mean, I'm not a lick player. I don't go around trying to do that. I never wanted to be, and that created problems for me growing up in Detroit. (ibid.)

Clearly, Alice's musical open-mindedness and willingness to depart from the restrictions of Detroit's bebop tradition, even in those early years, were indicative of the creative potential that she would unleash in her work with John Coltrane as well as in her own solo career.

When Alice's future husband came to Detroit's Minor Key in January 1962, Alice and Bennie Maupin attended the show together. Although Alice had heard John Coltrane with Miles Davis in Paris, it was the first time she had heard him live with his own ensemble. Maupin described their inspirational evening and the way in which the innovations of John Coltrane were quite challenging for Detroit audiences dedicated to the bebop style:

The music just overwhelmed us. I mean, we got there—I went and picked her up and we drove over to this place, and it used to be an old furniture store. So they had an area that you could kind of sit in upstairs, so we were able to get upstairs and sit right in front of the bandstand, so we could look right down at the band. And we sat there all night, you know, and just listened to that music, you know? But even prior to that, going to hear John live, we were already daily listening to *Africa Brass* and just marveling at what had happened there. No one had made a recording like that. You know, with that kind of intensity, with the sounds of animals, and you know, it was just, it was just very different. But that was a very special night for us that I'll never forget, because we sat there and we listened to the music, and people were very—the Detroit audience was very oriented towards bebop, to say the least, which is why so many great bebop players come from there—and, you know, they loved John's music, and a lot of people were connected to John, of course, through Miles. But as he started to come with his own music, people started to be very critical. And people were not so easy to relax and say, "oh yeah, he's just reaching for something different." People were very, very vocal about how they, how the music had affected them. And they were, like, "what the hell is he doing?" You know, and so we sat there that night and we listened and we talked and we listened. We stayed the entire night. (ibid.)

On the Road with Terry Gibbs

In 1962, after Alice reestablished herself in Detroit, her childhood mentor Terry Pollard approached her about playing in Terry Gibbs's band. A New York bebopper and one of America's foremost vibraphone players at the time, Gibbs preferred to work with musicians from Detroit, who, he felt, possessed the necessary combination of dexterity, blues phrasing, and harmonic sophistication that his music required. Before hiring Alice, Gibbs had toured with a host of Detroit natives: Alice's half-brother, the bassist Ernest Farrow; the bassist Herman Wright; and the pianist Terry Pollard.

Alice's parents were aging, and although she was reluctant to leave her daughter Michelle and go on the road, Alice felt that it was time for her to get greater professional exposure, to ensure that she could better provide for herself. She auditioned for Terry Gibbs in New York at Nola's Studio and, according to Gibbs, "right from the introduction Alice played on the first song, I knew that she was something else. She sounded like Bud Powell. She played chorus after chorus, and every note was a gem" (Gibbs and Ginell 2003, 228).

Between 1962 and 1963, Alice toured the country with Gibbs's band, which at the time included Herman Wright on bass and Bobby Pike on drums. Their first big engagement was at the Metropole, in Manhattan, playing opposite Gene Krupa. In Gibbs's band, Alice made use of the mallet skills she had acquired in high school. She and Gibbs would "close the show with a duet, a kind of show business thing," which he had popularized earlier when Terry Pollard was in the band. Although Gibbs was a notorious entertainer, Alice was far more than a novelty act or "girl musician" for Gibbs:

> She wouldn't have been there if she couldn't play, because I don't hire anybody—girls, boys, yellows, blacks, greens—I only hire people that can play good and that I have fun playing with. She kept getting better all the time. We started out playing slowly, and as we played more and more, she got better and we played faster. She would have been a great vibes player if she had stayed with us. (Gibbs, telephone interview with author, 2001)

Later that summer, the band opened for the John Coltrane Quartet at New York's Birdland. It was during this engagement that Alice and John began to get to know one another. Gibbs recalled: "There was a back booth in Birdland where musicians could sit, and every time we'd get off the stage, Alice would be there, just staring at John while he played. I think she was falling in love with him" (ibid.). In our interview, Alice offered more details of her initial encounter with John Coltrane at Birdland:

> I had an inner feeling about him, but I'm not the only one—there must be thousands of people. When I heard his recordings I would hear not only what goes into your intelligence or your senses, your mentality—but also something else, like an-

other message. I connected with this other message. It was like he had to be saying that to me. Of course, that could be just the imagination. But I was connecting with another message that I perceived as coming though his music. So then when we were there at Birdland, and he was in performance, that same feeling would come back, like some kind of inner knowing, or recognizing something that I'm hearing, something that I comprehend was associated with my soul or spirit. I would think the first two days it wasn't more than you speak. That's it, "hello." And you just go sit down and don't have anything to say. He was the most quiet person! Quiet as quiet. His silence was loud because it was so pervasive—like he didn't hear anything. This little waiting room that the musicians would sit in before their performance, I don't believe it took up more space than around twelve by five or something. But he would sit there and the quiet was strong. It didn't make you feel isolated, but part of. I identified with it right away. And it was a kind of silence that you don't want to disturb. You don't interrupt with, "Oh, would you like some tea?" You respect it.

The first several days I had very little to say beyond "hello." That's it. When more than "hello" came out, well, I was walking into my little room, and I heard him play something that he had composed. He was walking behind me playing. I said, "This is so beautiful. What a very beautiful theme, a very beautiful melody." He said, "It's for you!" I said, "Thank you very much. It is so beautiful." From that moment on, from the moment that words were shared and exchanged—by the end of the week, well it was the termination of my time with Terry Gibbs. (A. Coltrane, interview with author, 2001)

After their stint working at Birdland in the summer of 1963, John would come to see Alice while she was on the road. Following a successful six-week tour on the West Coast and a reunion show in Detroit in 1964 that brought veteran Terry Pollard out to play, Alice quite suddenly resigned from Gibbs's band. Gibbs recalled in the book he wrote with Ginell:

About five days before we were to open at the London House, Alice came to me and said that John wanted her to go to Sweden with him and that they were eventually going to get married. I really got bugged because I had always wanted to play the London House. I was ready to call the union or my attorney. How could she do this to me? We had a winner and now she was going to leave me with an unrehearsed group. We had been together for almost one year. After calming down and thinking about it, I figured, to start with, how do you stop a woman in love from doing anything? Plus, Alice was one of the nicest people I ever knew. I lucked out by hiring Walter Bishop Jr., a very well known bebop piano player and we did very well at the London House. To this day, Alice and I are good friends. She lives about five miles from where I live and we talk to each other from time to time. (ibid., 231)

Straight Ahead

Alice's encounter with John Coltrane at Birdland in 1963 ultimately determined the course of her personal and artistic life. Listening to Coltrane improvise each night also inspired her musicianship in an immediate fashion. Her musical conception during this period is documented on three albums with Gibbs's band: *The Family Album* (1963), *El Nutto* (1964), and *Jewish Melodies in Jazztime* (1963), a rather forward-looking fusion album that brought the best New York klezmer musicians out of the woodwork to play. These LPs with Terry Gibbs provide the first commercial recordings of Alice's piano work prior to her collaborations with John Coltrane. They are also the only recordings available of her playing in the modern jazz idiom, as she abandoned the formal constraints of straight-ahead jazz in 1965, when she joined her husband's ensemble. For the most part, the structures of the original Gibbs compositions on these albums follow a thirty-two-bar AABA form, or a twelve-bar blues form, and display chord progressions and substitutions characteristic of bebop jazz. However, several tunes featured on *Jewish Melodies in Jazztime* are modal tunes that follow the harmonic structure of the Eastern European folk melodies that Gibbs drew upon.

The bebop idiom clearly pervades Alice's work here. One is immediately aware of the influence of her jazz mentors Barry Harris and Bud Powell, and the dominance of the bebop vocabulary popular among her Detroit peers. Parker-like chromatic phrases that accentuate chord tones frequently appear over the major chord, as in figure 1.1, taken from the first measure of her solo on "One for My Uncle," from *The Family Album.*[31] We see the same figure again, transposed with slight modification, in the first bar of her improvisation on "Henny Time," in figure 1.2. This phrase also appears in measure 27 of "Button Up your Lip" and in measures 1 and 5 of "Sunny Girl," as well as in several of her solos on the albums *El Nutto* and *Jewish Melodies in Jazztime.* Such highly calculated phrasing, the "licks" that players regularly rely on, is common in bebop-oriented playing, and individual musicians are known for their signature melodies.

Fig. 1.1 First measures of Coltrane's solo on "One for My Uncle."

Fig. 1.2 First bar of Coltrane's improvisation on "Henny Time."

Fig. 1.3 Measure 16 of Coltrane's solo in "Sunny Girl."

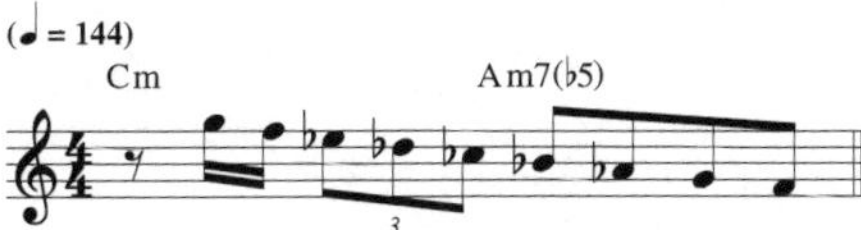

Fig. 1.4 First bar of Coltrane's solo on "Up at Louge's Place."

Fig. 1.5 Coltrane's "rhythm changes" bridge of Gibbs's "El Nutto."

Alice also employs the altered dominant scales that bebop musicians were using with great regularity by the late 1940s. The first is the whole-tone scale, often associated with Thelonious Monk, which is drawn from measure 16 of her solo in "Sunny Girl," shown in figure 1.3. Alice also favored the melodic minor scale, also known as the superlocrian, over dominant harmonies. Figure 1.4, taken from the first measure of her solo on "Up at Louge's Place," is a particularly salient use of this altered sonority, as it anticipates the actual dominant chord by one measure. This combination of horn-like bebop phrasing and her mastery of harmonic tension and release should remind listeners of her mentor Bud Powell. Also reminiscent of Powell are her lengthy phrases, made all the more interesting by the use of well-placed, highly syncopated accents. Observe, in figure 1.5, her masterful playing in the "rhythm changes" bridge of Gibbs's "El Nutto."

As was the case with many Detroit pianists, the blues idiom pervaded much of Alice's playing. One finds numerous examples of blues-based melodic elements, often in compound meter, which, though prevalent in mod-

Fig. 1.6 Measures 9–11 of Coltrane's solo on "El Cheapo."

Fig. 1.7 Measure 14 of "Henny Time."

ern jazz, are highly characteristic of the gospel genre. The church would also have been the context in which she absorbed and made use of this language from an early age, as opposed to the blues club or dance hall. For instance, figure 1.6, excerpted from measures 9–11 of her solo on "El Cheapo," demonstrates her frequent use of the ornamented pentatonic scale with a 12/8 feel. Blues aesthetics are also apparent in the note clusters she accents in her right hand. Jazz pianists use this device in order to imitate the blues inflections of guitar and voice; see, for example, figure 1.7, from measure 14 of "Henny Time."

Feeling over Form

Most noteworthy about Alice's style as an improviser during this period—what makes her truly distinct from her Motown colleagues—was the way that she infused Detroit's modern jazz language with a trance-like intensity. She regularly disrupted the formal and metrical aspects of Gibbs's compositions with extended modal passages and rhythmic and melodic motifs played over the bar line. Subdividing and expanding each beat, she achieved enormous feats of virtuosity. She committed herself so completely to the musical moment that formulaic patterns and preconceived ideas were ineffectual. Neither calculated nor predictable, her solos were inspired by "the dictates of the spirit," to borrow a phrase from Clarence Boyer.

For instance, with its precarious double-time passages and extended motivic development, her solo on "Up at Louge's Place" from *The Family Album* abandons the constraints of the meter and bar line and displays her predilection for feeling over form. The moments of emotional abandon heard on *The Family Album* anticipate even more ecstatic improvisations featured in the minor, modal tunes of *Jewish Melodies in Jazztime.* Tunes with static harmony provide for a much more intuitive and somatic improvising experience at the piano than do those with rapid harmonic motion. In such modal contexts, Alice allowed her technique to take over as she surrendered fully to rhythmic and motivic inspiration. She was also particularly at home in minor keys, especially improvising on tunes with slow harmonic motion—much of the music she recorded during her career as a bandleader, such as "Ptah the El Daoud" or "Journey in Satchidanda" were tunes of this nature. On *Jewish Melodies in Jazztime*, we can see that her improvisations were already headed in this direction. We can also begin to understand why John Coltrane may have been attracted to her playing. Gibbs recounted how Alice actually "stole the date" from him:

> She was starting to play runs she got from listening to John and all the musicians flipped out every time she played. She was making those Eastern-style runs on minor songs and they sounded very authentic. I was the Jew, and she was wiping me out. (2003, 230)

Salient aspects of this virtuosity can be seen in the opening bars of her solo on "Bei Mir Bist du Schon." There she introduced a double-time motif that outlined the interval of a third. She later repeated and transposed this figure, thereby obscuring the beat, barline, and harmony of the original tune. Figure 1.8 shows the opening measure of her solo, followed by measures 12–18 in figure 1.9.

There is a shimmering intensity in her double-time work on this album that results from the ornamentation and varieties of rhythms she used, even

Fig. 1.8 Opening measure of Coltrane's solo on "Bei Mir Bist du Schon."

Fig. 1.9 Measures 12–18 of "Bei Mir Bist du Schon."

Fig. 1.10 Opening measure of "Nyah Shere."

Fig. 1.11 Measures 33–34 of "Shaine Une Zees."

at breakneck tempos. She was also an extremely nimble pianist—John Coltrane used the adjective "fleet" to describe her playing. Notice the gestural nature and rhythmic complexity of her opening statement on "Nyah Shere" (figure 1.10) and measures 33–34 from "Shaine Une Zees" (figure 1.11).

What we see in Alice's early tracks with Terry Gibbs is not the work of a young novice, but that of a seasoned musician already disposed toward the emotional, technical, and spiritual intensity that would come to define her playing with her husband. Raised in a religious and exceptionally musical household in postwar Detroit, Alice was slated for early professional success. Close family ties to Detroit's gospel and bebop network gave her access to playing opportunities, insider knowledge of the latest techniques and innovations, and a comparatively stress-free environment as a female musician. As a church musician, Alice drew from a rich well of African American folk music and ritual performance practices that date back to slavery. As a progressive bebop musician, she was also up to date on the latest rhythmic and harmonic innovations occurring among her peers. Finally, she was deeply influenced by the musical and spiritual ecstasy of gospel worship, elements she felt were present in the music of John Coltrane. All of these aspects would coalesce into a definitive, original, and mature artistic concept during her years as John Coltrane's musical and spiritual partner.

John and Alice Coltrane. Rudy Van Gelder's studio, 1967.
Photo courtesy of Chuck Stewart

Alice Coltrane. Rudy Van Gelder's studio, 1967. *Photo courtesy of Chuck Stewart*

Alice Coltrane and Swami Satchitananda. Rishikesh, India, 1968.
Photo courtesy of Integral Yoga

Alice Coltrane with harp, January 1970. *Photo courtesy of Chuck Stewart*

Eternity album cover, 1975. *Photo courtesy of Warner Brothers/ Rhino Entertainment*

Transcendence album cover, 1977. *Photo courtesy of Warner Brothers/ Rhino Entertainment*

Radha Krsna Nama Sankirtana album cover, 1977. *Photo courtesy of Warner Brothers/Rhino Entertainment*

Alice Coltrane with harp. Warsaw, 1987. *Photo courtesy of Hans Kumpf*

Alice Coltrane at the keyboard. Warsaw, 1987. *Photo courtesy of Hans Kumpf*

CHAPTER TWO

Manifestation

Of course, John Coltrane is the one who inspires everybody, if you were fortunate enough to be in his presence in those days. He would always encourage you to fully express what you had. Not half of it, because it's not made that way, or three-quarters—the entire experience of the expressive self. Truth on your instrument. That just opens so many doors, so many avenues, so many vistas, so many plateaus. You could hear your sound, music, light coming from the ethereal, heavenly realms. When you played in octaves that you would never go—your bass area, and your contrabass area, or your tenor area. You heard all kinds of things that would have just been left alone, never a part of your discovery or appreciation. —Alice Coltrane

In February 1966, Alice McLeod, now Alice Coltrane, made her first recording with her husband John in a San Francisco studio, which was posthumously issued as "Manifestation" on the CD *Cosmic Music*. Her stunning and seemingly overnight transformation from a Detroit bebop pianist to a champion of the new music evident on this recording speaks to the profound impact of John Coltrane as a musical role model. It also raises the question of how she acquired these new techniques. She had not been participating at jam sessions or performing club dates devoted to free jazz. To the contrary, shortly after Alice McLeod and John Coltrane met at Birdland in July 1963, they began their life together as a family, and she gave up steady work as a musician. While she was touring, Alice had asked her aunt to care for Alice's daughter, Michelle. Now, after a joyful reunion with Michelle, Alice soon found herself pregnant. She and John had three boys within three years: John Junior, 1964–85; Ravi, born 1965; and Oran, born in 1967).[1] Her discography indicates this dramatic turn of events, with its gap of two and a half years between her last studio session with Terry Gibbs and her 1966 recording debut with her husband.

In 1966 when Alice recorded "Manifestation," it was not clear that she would become John Coltrane's regular pianist. However, soon after the

February recording session, John asked her to join his new group, featuring Rashied Ali on drums, Jimmy Garrison on bass, and Pharoah Sanders on woodwinds. This was a highly controversial decision in the jazz world: John Coltrane's previous "classic quartet," featuring the pianist McCoy Tyner and the drummer Elvin Jones, had won him great public notoriety. Tyner's distinctive and innovative approach as an accompanist had also been crucial to John Coltrane's artistic development. For any pianist, these would have been large shoes to fill.[2] Furthermore, John was exploring extremely dissonant, free-form musical templates that were alienating many of his fans. As Alice put it: "When he became avant-garde, as they termed it, he lost many people, many followers. They didn't like it, they didn't approve of it, they didn't appreciate it. And there was no way he could go back, there was no road to return to. It was his commitment, it was his decision" (A. Coltrane, interview with Palmer, 1991).

Despite the controversy surrounding the dissolution of his previous all-star band, the direction of his new music, and the serious health problems that emerged during the last year and a half of his life, John Coltrane recorded a significant amount of material with Alice and his quintet, with the support of Bob Theile and the Impulse! label. Nearly all of this music was issued posthumously, and a good portion has only recently been released. Fortunately, there is now substantial documentation of John's late work and Alice's musical contributions to her husband's ensemble, which can be heard on the albums *Cosmic Music*, recorded 1966–68; *Live at the Village Vanguard Again!* 1966; *Live in Japan*, 1966; *Expression*, 1967; *Stellar Regions*, 1967; and *The Olatunji Concert*, 1967.

Clearly, John Coltrane had a profound influence on Alice's musicianship. Even though she had not been on stage for many months, she had been immersed in her husband's music, so that when she joined him in the recording studio, she was attuned to his compositional sensibilities. Furthermore, Coltrane was an effective and encouraging bandleader who always achieved tremendous results from his players. Playing solos on John's compositions, Alice was no longer constrained by meters, bar lines, or fixed harmonic indications. She integrated the blues-based pentatonic language of her prior style with rapidly shifting tonic pedals and extreme dissonance. Freed from the formal mandates of bebop, she made full use of her technical prowess and the entire range of the piano, expressing herself without reservation. She allowed the "dictates of the spirit" that surfaced in her work with Terry Gibbs to fully "manifest" themselves (Boyer 1995, 44).

Although John taught Alice—as he did all his band members—to fully explore her creative potential, it is important to realize that their relationship was not simply one of musical mentor and disciple: it was an intimate and complex marital partnership, in which family life and religious exploration provided a foundation for their mutual development. In fact, I believe that John Coltrane's biographers have significantly underestimated Alice's deep influence on him as a partner. In the short time that they were together (July 1963 to July 1967), John Coltrane's music changed dramatically. When the couple first met in Birdland in 1963, he was performing with his classic quintet and straddling a somewhat conservative middle ground between the metered, modal music of the jazz mainstream and the timbral explorations of the avant-garde. In 1965, however, he assembled a new group for the album *Ascension* and was committed almost exclusively thereafter to playing "free."[3] When Alice joined him on the bandstand after her three-year maternal leave, he recorded the albums listed above, six of the most unconventional and daring projects of his career. Furthermore, the spiritual intent of his music, first revealed in *A Love Supreme* in 1965 and in later "out" recordings such as *Om* (1965) and *Meditation* (1966), became increasingly explicit during his time with Alice. It was also at this time that he gained the reputation of jazz guru.

Remarkably, despite both her prior immersion in the church and her subsequent life as a swami and devotional musician, Alice has largely been left out of the accepted account of her husband's spiritual rebirth during the 1960s. But this should not come as a surprise. Even at the height of her own commercial recording career, Alice never received recognition commensurate with her contributions; in the public's imagination, she remained, and still remains, simply the wife of John Coltrane. Alice herself was partly responsible for this lack of recognition. She was always self-effacing in interviews and behaved with the conviction that service to her husband's legacy was historically important. Journalists and scholars rarely asked Alice about her own career. Instead, they viewed her as a primary source of information about her late husband. This problem plagues all of Coltrane's former sidemen; however, Alice's status as significant other—privy to the man behind the horn—has exacerbated this problem. Moreover, she privately and publicly embraced her role as partner and feminine counterpart to her husband: "I kind of liked housekeeping myself. I liked to cook. I liked being a mother. I liked having a house. I liked all of that part of it" (interview with author, 2001).

This is not to say that she was unaware of the workings of male power or the prevailing attitudes of the women's liberation movement. Rather, she asserted a feminist politics of interdependence as opposed to one that would have women become more like men. If she had had a different attitude, she might never have found the innovative and complementary style as a side person that she did in her husband's late quintet. In a 1988 radio interview with Dolores Brandon, Alice explained:

Can I just state that I do believe that men feel this is their world. And it's true that they have been endowed with male power. And that male power is quite analytical and technical and I think it best manifests when it is inventive and creative. And, I have noticed that instead of being inventive and creative, often it's not that. It's negative. And I wouldn't think that it would be negative if what they really expressed in male power was to be leaders and teachers and guides and things like this. I mean they really are endowed. But when they turn it into themselves to control the world, to control people, and then females! They don't have a very positive view of her. Often they have utilized her, you see what I mean. They've never, well not ever, I can't say this, but they don't seem to promote womanhood or uplift womanhood. And that's what I admired about John so much. He uplifted it here. He respected it. It was wife, mother of his children. It was mate. It was friend. And really, I didn't want to be equal to him. I didn't have to be equal to him and do what he did. That, I never considered. I don't think like that. And whatever in the women's liberation—that's what they want. I didn't want to be equal to him. I wanted to be a wife, to be that for him, that part of him. (A. Coltrane 1988)

Alice further elaborated on how shared family and spiritual life provided a basis for their mutual musical growth:

He, I felt, brought out the best in me musically, as his wife and mother of his children. Somehow he was also inspired to bring out the avant-garde music. I feel that it was always in him, being born with this gift, this God-given gift of music. It was there. Of course over the years, we heard it. We would hear these ways, these wonderful sounds coming from him. *To me, as result of the association* [their marriage], *it fully manifested. There was no more question about direction.* (ibid., emphasis mine)

Responding to these statements, Brandon asked, "Do you think it had something to do with the birth of the children as well?" Alice answered:

I think all of it is a part of it because he was always inspired. He was very much a family man, always at home, if he was not traveling and concertizing. I do believe that all of those factors contributed to his higher involvement, his higher innovation in music . . . As a result of our association, I saw him more one-pointed, focused in the direction he was going without question. I think there were questionings from others around him, associates, musicians. But he seemed to focus on his goals with a conviction. *What we did was really to begin to reach out and look toward higher experiences in spiritual life and higher knowledge to be obtained in spiritual life. This is what we did. And our basic root was, of course, reading and hearing discourse, talk by spiritual leaders and teachers, as well as our own engagement in meditation.* (ibid., emphasis mine)

Alice and John Coltrane shared a desire "to reach out and look toward higher experiences in spiritual life." As a couple, they explored a variety of non-Western religious traditions and embraced the transcendent potential of jazz improvisation; these pursuits as a couple ultimately laid the foundation for Alice's subsequent spiritual journey and the musical aesthetics she developed during her career as a bandleader. Their pursuits were also deeply embedded in the religious culture of the 1960s. Alice's future artistic transformation and the spiritually oriented aesthetics of her late-modal and free-jazz explorations with her husband are best viewed in the context of this exploratory religious zeitgeist.

John Coltrane's Spiritual Jazz

Although his canonical status as jazz guru—a reputation cemented by the platinum-selling album *A Love Supreme (*1965)—belies the fact, John Coltrane was not the first jazz musician to draw on spiritual subject matter for musical inspiration. Other famous jazz composers, such as Duke Ellington and Charles Mingus, had alluded to the black church much earlier in their respective works "The Black and Tan Fantasy" and "Prayer Meeting." In the 1950s, this trend became increasingly popular as hard-bop players drew consistently from the gospel genre in order to differentiate and reclaim their music from that of the white "cool school."[4] It has by now become rather standard in both jazz scholarship and popular music forums to link black secular musical aesthetics to church practices, jazz not withstanding.[5]

Significantly less attention, however, has been paid to the influence of non-Christian religious affiliations among African Americans and how those ties have also had an impact on aesthetics. This is despite the fact that as early as the 1940s, many influential and innovative jazz musicians began to follow Islam and other non-Christian practices: the Detroit native Yusef Lateef converted to Ahmadiyya Islam in the early 1950s, as did the drummer Art Blakey; and McCoy Tyner was a Sunni Muslim for a period of time in the mid-1950s.[6] By the 1960s, jazz musicians were drawing consistently from not only African American spiritual traditions and Islamic practices, but also East Asian and South Asian religions, as well as idiosyncratic spiritual concepts.[7] Clearly, such musical and spiritual explorations of the East, Africa, and various cosmic realms distanced jazz from the traditional Protestant church as the locus of black ethnicity. Nevertheless, many of the same "functional dimensions" of African American sacred music persisted, to use Mellonee Burnim's useful term. The new spiritual jazz continued to provide "a means of cultural affirmation, individual and collective expression, and spiritual sustenance" (Burnim 1988, 112).

Although jazz musicians referred to the black church and other religious practices in their music prior to John Coltrane, his spiritual impact in this regard was singular: he imbued the modal and avant-garde jazz improvisation of the 1960s with spiritual significance, and, in many respects, he succeeded in creating a new religion for jazz musicians based on what Alice described as "the entire experience of the expressive self" (interview with author, 2001). John encouraged Alice and his other band members to make extraordinarily personal statements. While the authenticity that he sought—"the entire experience of the expressive self" and "truth on your instrument"—was intrinsic to his spiritual philosophy, it also had extensive political ramifications during the civil rights era as a display of personal liberation and black cultural expression. Let me quote again Alice's recollection of playing with her husband:

> Of course, John Coltrane is the one who inspires everybody, if you were fortunate enough to be in his presence in those days. He would always encourage you to fully express what you had. Not half of it, because it's not made that way, or three-quarters—the entire experience of the expressive self. Truth on your instrument. That just opens so many doors, so many avenues, so many vistas, so many plateaus. You could hear your sound, music, light, coming from the ethereal, heavenly realms. When you played in octaves that you would never go—your bass area, and your contrabass area, or your tenor area. You heard all kinds of things that would have just been left alone, never a part of your discovery or appreciation. (ibid.)

It is of great significance that John Coltrane's spiritual vision was inspired by a concept of a supreme being more universal and inclusive than that of the Judeo-Christian tradition of his childhood. By the early 1960s, Coltrane found strength and solace in a well-reasoned, nonsectarian view of God, which Lewis Porter calls "a kind of universal religion" (1998, 211). Included in his spirituality was an array of world traditions: Zen, Zoroastrianism, the writings of Yogananda and Krishnamurti, and a commitment to daily meditation, all of which he explored with Alice.

By the early 1960s, John Coltrane's "universal spirituality" became increasingly fused with his interest in world music, and he developed a multicultural theory of musical transcendence that had a lasting impact on Alice's later career.[8] In an interview with Nat Hentoff in 1961, Coltrane stated, "I've already been looking into those approaches to music, as in India in which particular scales are intended to produce specific emotional meanings" (quoted in Hentoff 1961). Coltrane was particularly fascinated with the music of the sitar player Ravi Shankar, after whom he named his second son. Shankar began concertizing in the West in the early 1950s and almost single-handedly popularized Indian classical music in America, inspiring a great many jazz musicians of the era.[9] Coltrane had also befriended the Nigerian drummer Babatunde Olatunji, one of the first proponents of West African traditional music in America, with whom he would speak at great length about the relationship between African tonal languages and drumming patterns.[10] In the summer of 1963, the same summer he met Alice, John Coltrane discussed his interest in the magical, healing properties of music in an interview with French journalists (J. Coltrane 1963, 14).

The timing was perfect for Coltrane's unique synthesis. The modal jazz forms that he had pioneered with the Miles Davis sextet during the late 1950s allowed for the superimposition of non-Western music. The static harmony and tonic pedals that defined modal jazz—found on Davis's albums such as the 1958 *Milestones* and the 1959 *Kind of Blue*—allowed for the incorporation of music that relied on a drone, or an unchanging tonal center, a device common in Asian and African music. By the late 1960s, John Coltrane's concept of musical transcendence was extraordinarily popular. His fans and fellow musicians had come to associate his spiritual views with the compositional devices he used on the album *A Love Supreme* and in other recordings from this period. Mantra-like melodies, static harmonies, pentatonic improvisations, dynamic ensemble interactions, and increasing freedom from metric constraints came to signify both a religious attitude and a new ecstatic spiritual practice in its own right. One should keep in mind, however, that John Coltrane never applied non-Western musical genres in an orthodox manner: he took aspects of these traditions and absorbed them into his own jazz-based modal structures. With their attendant transcendent or healing properties, these non-Western sources were filtered through a personal musical and spiritual philosophy of expressing inner truth. In short, John Coltrane's creative ideology was deeply intertwined with his spiritual philosophy, which rested on three basic tenets and which Alice fully embraced. First, music making is based on personal spiritual expression, and the artist should be fully committed to expressing an authentic self as a musician. Second, music making should be universal, erasing aesthetic boundaries and proscriptions about style. And third, such musical universality requires branching out: it is inclusive, pluralistic, and multicultural.[11]

Sixties Spirituality

The personalized, eclectic, and global nature of John Coltrane's spiritual and creative ideology was consistent with the new religious culture of the 1960s. Religion scholars have observed a profound transformation in American spirituality during the era. Religious identities that had long been rooted in "social sources of denominationalism," such as class, region, race, and ethnicity, began to deteriorate as a product of greater social mobility in the period after the Second World War.[12] Prior to mid-century, communities worshiped together "in ethnic enclaves that gave religious practice a distinct geographic identity" (Wuthnow 1998, 23). This earlier model was one in which "family, church, and neighborhood were closely integrated" (20). By the 1960s, this "spirituality of dwelling" had given way "to a new spirituality of seeking," in which individuals began to "increasingly negotiate among competing glimpses of the sacred" (3).

Religious practice of the 1960s also became more "inwardly focused": the "search for the spiritual went beyond doctrine, creed, or religion" and was concerned instead with "an inner world of truth and meaning" and "individualized authentic identity" (Roof 1999, 66). The philosopher Charles Taylor sees this as part of America's "culture of authenticity," tracing its roots to the rational and political individualism of Descartes and Rousseau, the heartfelt yearnings of the Romantics, the "committed inwardness" of Protestant Christianity, and Herder's eighteenth-century notion that people had individual "essences." As Taylor puts it:

> Being true to myself means being true to my own originality, and that is something that only I can articulate and discover. In articulating it, I am also defining myself. I am realizing a potentiality that is properly my own. This is the background understanding to the modern ideal of authenticity, and to the goals of self-fulfillment or self-realization in which it is usually couched. (Taylor 1992, 29)

According to Taylor, this Western notion of "being true to myself" was connected to a political and spiritual "horizon of significance" during the 1960s, so that individual expressive acts could "offer a picture of what a better or higher life would be" and set "a standard of what we ought to desire" (ibid.).

However, another form of individualism should also be considered with respect to jazz avant-garde jazz, as it impinges on Taylor's framework in important ways. Expressing individuality is a fundamental aspect of African American musical aesthetics. Scholars trace such musical features as the importance of the soloist within the collective, improvisation, and the requirement of having "your own sound" to premodern West Africa, not the modern West.[13] Many of these musical traditions define jazz, its avant-garde variants notwithstanding. Furthermore, acknowledging these African musical origins was central to the spiritual jazz culture of the 1960s.

Scholars have also observed a renewed interest in Asian religions and their American cousins, sometimes called harmonial or metaphysical religions. During the 1960s, Eastern spiritual traditions were explored with new vigor—facilitated, in part, by the Asian Immigration Act of 1965, which led South and East Asians to bring their daily religious practices to U.S. soil.[14] Technological advances, postwar affluence, and the media focus on foreign wars of liberation also produced a new global exchange in which "religious symbols, teachings, and practices" were easily "disembedded" and "reembedded" into one another, resulting in "religious pluralism within the individual," "bricolage," and a "mixing of codes" (Roof 1999, 73).

These trends in mainstream America held true for black America as well. However, the role of religion and the presence of religious leaders in the struggle for civil rights brought a new urgency to the issue of black spirituality. To quote Gayraud Wilmore, the late 1960s was "an unprecedented era of black theological reflection" (1998, 244). The political efficacy of the mainstream Protestant church was a topic of enormous debate. Proponents saw the church as the wellspring of all black institutions, and one of the richest elements in black culture and social organization (Frazier 1964; Fichter 1965). They viewed the 1960s as a renaissance in which the church could resume its traditional functions of challenging the goals of white America. Critics, however, complained that the church no longer lived up to the expectations engendered in its past, and that its fragmentation and complacency had led it to abandon the black underclass, which was facing ever-increasing economic and political hardship (Washington 1964; Clark 1964; Cleage 1972).

These debates were contemporaneous with the rise of new forms of Afrocentric spirituality associated with cultural nationalism: some examples are Ron Karenga's Kwanzaa; an interest in Egyptology, as well as in forms of black religion such as Santeria; and, of course, the rise of the Nation of Islam. The expansion and assertion of black spirituality, however, was not limited to a return to African roots. For some black Americans, the new spirituality included a journey East to Japan or India, and into the realms of meditation and yoga.

This assertion of spirituality, even eclectic and Asian spirituality, was in keeping with the politics of Black Power. Though Black Power is typically associated with the political concerns of African American economic development, education, and even armed self-defense, it was also concerned with defining and asserting blackness as a cultural ideal. This, in turn, required a new spiritual foundation. Members of the Black Arts movement—the cultural arm of the Black Power movement—wrote ardently about the need for a black spiritual culture whose politics were consistent with the revolutionary agenda of Black Nationalism. In 1969, writing on the theme of spirituality emerging in the plays of Black Arts literary figures, Larry Neal asserted:

> The Old Spirituality is generalized. It seeks to recognize Universal Humanity. The New Spirituality is specific. It begins by seeing the world from the concise point of view of the colonialized. Where the Old Spirituality would live with Oppression while ascribing to the oppressors an innate goodness, the New Spirituality demands a radical shift in point of view. The colonized native, the oppressed must, of necessity, subscribe to a separate morality. One that will liberate him and his people. (1989, 77)

In an essay called “The Religion of Black Power,” Vincent Harding enthusiastically proclaimed that “Allah and other gods of Africa enter into competition with Yahweh, Jesus, and Buddha . . . It is joyously difficult but part of the affirmation of Black Power that ‘we are a spiritual people’” (1968, 30). That this simple, unequivocal assertion of spirituality was not necessarily bound to Africa as a cultural or geographic homeland opened the possibility of myriad forms that religion and spirituality could take. “We are a spiritual people” was also frequently coupled with what Wilmore describes as “a new pride in the strange and wonderful beauty of being black and letting it all hang out” (1998, 225).

The cultural historian Melani McAlister has written persuasively on the political dimensions of African Americans’ interest in non-Western religions.[15] McAlister sees such spiritual explorations among black Americans as a way of forming “an alternative sacred geography” that provides “alternatives to official policy, framing transnational affiliations and claims to racial or religious authority that challenged the cultural logic of American power.” She sees these spiritual pursuits as part of a larger project that encompasses “a re-visioning of history and geography in order to construct a moral and spiritual basis for contemporary affiliations and identities” (1999, 638). In her words:

> The attempt to construct a new black culture was deeply intertwined with the search for religious alternatives to mainstream Christianity, a search that included not only Islam, but also a renewed interest in the signs and symbols of pre-Islamic and traditional African religions (such as the Yoruban religion) and the study of ancient Egypt. These influences were often mixed together . . . in an eclectic, sometimes deliberately mystical, mix. (ibid.)

Drawing on the work of Pierre Bourdieu, McAlister argues that cultural productions make meaning by their “historical association with other types of meaning-making activity” (2001, 8). She says that we need to “‘explain the coincidence’ that brings specific cultural products into conversation with specific discourses” (7). While Alice and John Coltrane were not explicit about the transnational politics of their music or spirituality, when framed within the “alternative sacred geography” of the Black Arts movement, their avant-garde explorations are rendered politically meaningful.

Alice and the Late Quintet

In May 1966, John Coltrane’s new quintet was scheduled for a live recording at the Village Vanguard, in New York and John offered Alice the position as pianist in his band. At first, she did not feel up to the task and was hesitant to join: "I didn't know whether to accept . . . because I'm considering there are so many other people who'd be more qualified" (quoted in Toop 2002, 40). But soon she was making powerful, compelling statements in these new avant-garde musical environments. In fact, she never went back to playing typical twelve-bar and thirty-two-bar tunes. In an interview in the 1980s, she reflected on her musical transformation with her husband and the lasting appeal of avant-garde improvisation:

I really was quite conventional. I wasn't innovative or exploratory. I saw music as conforming to the basic chord progressions that were being played by so many musicians around the country . . . I do not dislike it [the old style] but I prefer avant-garde music because it isn't as restrictive . . . If you're set in this 12-bar pattern, you don't change from that; you stay within that confinement. For people with limited ability, maybe it's a safety measure to play in that context. But for innovative people, that's quite limiting . . . Avant-garde music to me is like journeying across the country until you come to a beautiful park. You say, "We'll stop here for just a moment." After a while you decide to go onward because you know of a nice area ahead, but before you leave, you see a lake that you didn't notice before, and you decide to stay and experience that for a while. Sometimes your moment is there like an eternity. This type of thing is quite prevalent in my music. (quoted in Lerner 1982, 24)

In some respects, improvising on John Coltrane's late compositions required that Alice chart very new territory. The expressive intensity and adventuresome nature of his musical templates called for a very different kind of musicianship than the three-minute bebop solos she had previously recorded as a side person with Terry Gibbs: John wished to do away with the conventions of fixed meter, fixed formal structure, and standard harmonic progressions. In both his original tunes and his reinterpretations of standard material, he would minimally suggest a melody, a mode or modes, and a texture, and then let his players explore their wider implications. Often, one rendition of a piece could last as long as forty-five minutes, and it was not unusual for individual solos to last twenty minutes.

One might imagine that such loosely structured environments require less skill on the part of the improviser; in fact, avant-garde forms demand great musicianship if the final results are to be successful. Gone are the "safety measures"—to use Alice's term—of the cyclical form, stock phrases, and the clear beginning, middle, and end of a tune. With parameters open and ample time to explore, the improviser must generate his or her own logic. Furthermore, musical statements must be unambiguous and interesting for ensemble interaction to progress.

While John's musical forms were different from anything that Alice had played before, her previous musical experiences had more than adequately prepared her. In her own band in Detroit in the early 1960s, and on the bandstand with Terry Gibbs, she had already explored modality in rather adventuresome ways. As a church keyboard player, she was accustomed to navigating loose formal structures that catered to "the dictates of the spirit," and she had developed the necessary mental and physical endurance. As a bebop player and devoted student of classical music, she had acquired technical abilities adequate to keep up with her husband's tempos. In short, playing with John Coltrane was not so much a break with her past as a Detroit pianist than it was an opportunity for Alice to fully realize the potential that had already emerged. John seemed convinced of this, even when Alice was not: "He said," she explained, "'You know you can do it, and I want you to.' His confidence in me was so strong. One day he said to me, 'This music is like a second nature to you. It's just like it's a part of you, a part of your life'" (quoted in Toop 2002, 40).

Ultimately, I believe that what made her musical transformation so smooth and surprisingly uncomplicated was that, even though the music she played with John Coltrane was avant-garde, she found herself in an extremely familiar musical situation. Given the spiritual intent of her husband's music and what he was trying to achieve on an expressive level, Alice was able to step into the familiar role of church accompanist. She was also performing with a close family member, as she had been throughout her earlier professional life.

Apparently, John did little instructing. Rather than rehearse his musicians in a conventional manner, he provided an open-ended musical environment that fostered experimentation and personal growth. According to Alice:

> There really was no practice. We didn't really practice together like certain people who have to have two or three rehearsals a week . . . He gave freedom to musicians to develop themselves within the music he was bringing out of them. He would talk about music rather than demonstrate what should be done and what should go where. He was that way with the other group [the previous quartet] as well as with us. (quoted in Lerner 1982, 23)

John did, however, offer general statements that helped Alice blossom as a soloist: "When I first joined the group I was struggling with the music. Because he was a master, he saw that I was playing with only a few octaves. He told me to play the whole piano, utilize the range so I wouldn't be locked in. It freed me" (A. Coltrane 1971, 42). For the most part, it seems that simply being in John Coltrane's artistic presence inspired Alice's very best playing:

> It was the kind of experience that words do not do justice to. There was no one I had seen or heard of on Earth with a mentality and knowledge of music like his, as

well as that genius level of creativity, and I still have not witnessed it anywhere else. Being with him in that kind of musical association, somehow there was no limit to how much you could excel. He inspired that kind of motivation, because there was so much freedom. He never said, "Don't play like this." I was encouraged to play the instrument fully, to give myself totally. (quoted in Lerner 1982, 23)

Listening to Alice's improvisations on her husband's free-form compositions, one might initially be struck by what seems a barrage of rapid-fire scales and glissandi. Even within these nonmetered, loosely tonal structures, however, there are several organizational principals at work that shape her solos, creating a sense of cohesion, punctuation, and excitement. "Manifestation," her first recorded improvisation with John Coltrane, provides a window into many of the techniques she employs on her husband's free-form compositions (see figure 2.1). Compared to her longer solos on live recordings, this three-minute miniature also offers a condensed version of her strategies as a soloist, and it is therefore a convenient place to begin a discussion of her playing in the Coltrane Quartet.

After John Coltrane's aggressive exploration of the timbral effects produced by the tenor saxophone, Alice begins her solo with a tremolo figure. Here, we immediately see her investigating the textural possibilities of the piano—one of her major areas of development as a player with John. This first section of her solo (indicated in figure 2.1 as BLOCK 1) calms the previous intensity created by John's dissonant explorations. She then plays a series of melodic cells with her right hand that suggests E major, while her left hand plays a repetitive figure in E major diatonic thirds. Soon, however, her diatonic left-hand intervals give way to rapidly shifting tritones and planning fourths (indicated as BLOCK 2). The sparseness of her left-hand voicing typifies the accompanimental techniques of modern jazz; her use of tritone shells is particularly characteristic of bebop and is prevalent in her earlier solos.

Her preference for perfect fourths in the left hand and the related pentatonic vocabulary in the right is unquestionably the inheritance of McCoy Tyner, who established the practice of using quartal harmonies in Coltrane's Classic Quintet. But Alice uses these fourth structures in a personal, mercurial manner; her constantly shifting left hand adds tremendous contrapuntal interest to her solos. This unpredictable quality distinguishes her playing from that of Tyner, who usually interjects rhythms in more regular time intervals. As a clear case in point, one can compare her left-hand playing with her husband on "My Favorite Things," recorded in 1966, with the popular version Tyner recorded with John Coltrane in 1960. Where Tyner keeps a steady waltz time, Alice obscures and again reestablishes the feeling of meter, which creates a sense of tension and release in her improvisation.

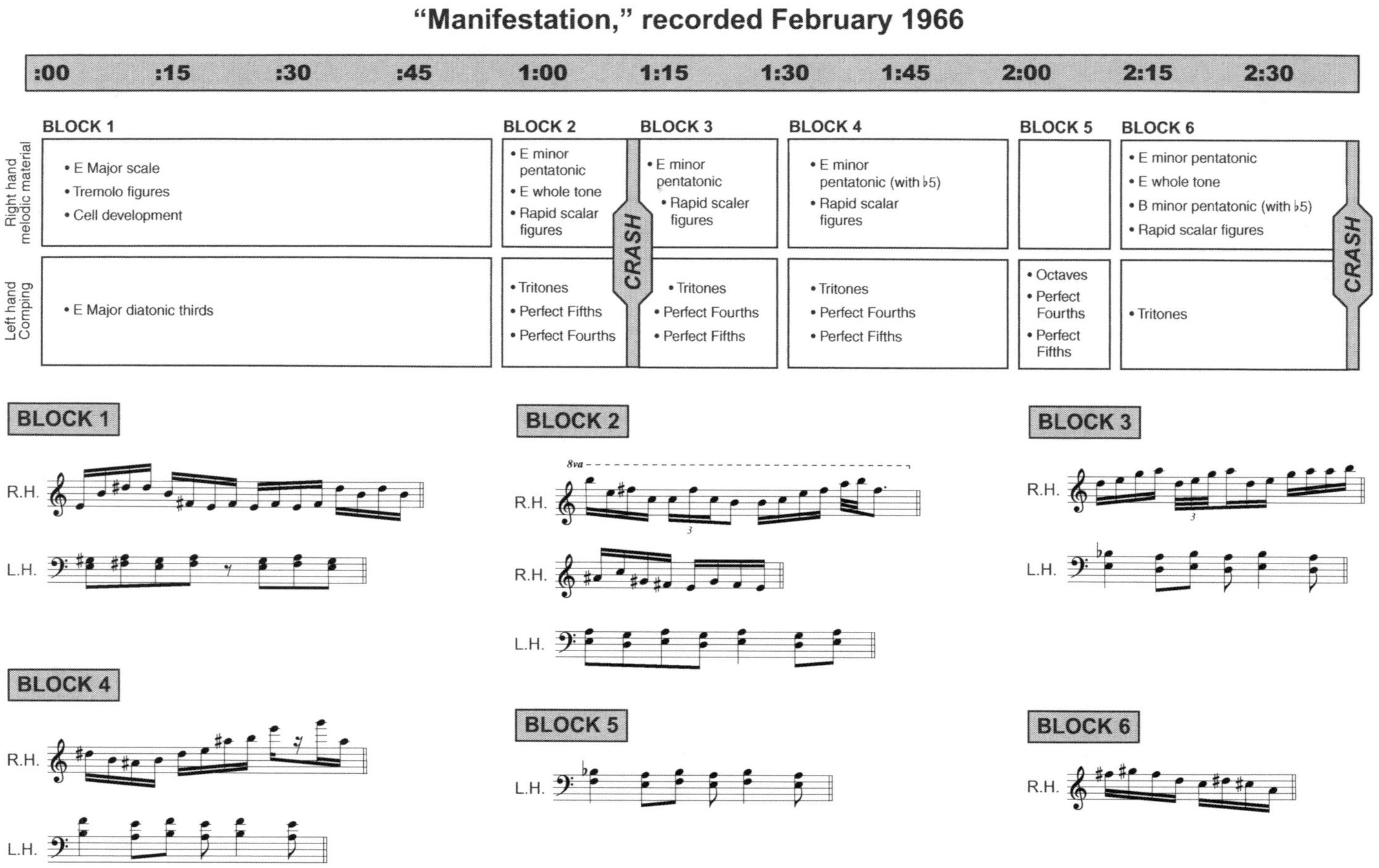
"Manifestation," recorded February 1966
:00
:15
:30
:45
1:00
1:15
1:30
1:45
2:00
2:15
2:30
Right hand melodic material
Left hand Comping
BLOCK 1
• E Major scale
• Tremolo figures
• Cell development
• E Major diatonic thirds
BLOCK 2
• E minor pentatonic
• E whole tone
• Rapid scalar figures
• Tritones
• Perfect Fifths
• Perfect Fourths
CRASH
BLOCK 3
• E minor pentatonic
• Rapid scaler figures
• Tritones
• Perfect Fourths
• Perfect Fifths
BLOCK 4
• E minor pentatonic (with ♭5)
• Rapid scalar figures
• Tritones
• Perfect Fourths
• Perfect Fifths
BLOCK 5
• Octaves
• Perfect Fourths
• Perfect Fifths
BLOCK 6
• E minor pentatonic
• E whole tone
• B minor pentatonic (with ♭5)
• Rapid scalar figures
• Tritones
CRASH
BLOCK 1
R.H.
L.H.
BLOCK 2
8va
R.H.
R.H.
L.H.
BLOCK 3
R.H.
L.H.
BLOCK 4
R.H.
L.H.
BLOCK 5
L.H.
BLOCK 6
R.H.

Fig. 2.1 Alice Coltrane's solos on "Manifestation."

Her ability to both swing at will and play in a more rhythmically abstract manner gives her an enormous range of expressive power here and elsewhere.

As her left-hand figures become increasingly abstract, her right hand melodies explore the gamut of E tonality, making use of scalar figures belonging to E minor, E minor pentatonic, and E whole tone, with nondiatonic embellishment. This motivic and modal right-hand vocabulary is reminiscent of her playing on Gibbs's tunes; however, with John Coltrane she is free to follow her inclinations without the bar-line interrupting her flow. As her solo progresses, her use of dissonance increases and she extends her range, playing simultaneously in the upper and lower octaves of the piano. At the height of musical intensity, Alice employs a crashing E pedal in the low register that grounds the solo and reestablishes the E tonality (indicated at the beginning of BLOCK 3 as CRASH). This low-register pedal technique acts as a punctuating device in her solos: in later pieces, it also serves to establish new tonal centers. Tyner boldly asserts octaves and fifths in this fashion; again, one of the better-known examples can be found on the 1960 recording of "My Favorite Things." Alice wisely borrows from Tyner's vocabulary here and uses this technique to rein in the frenetic energy of her own solos.

After reestablishing a sense of E minor, she moves again from simple to complex, employing increasing dissonance (indicated as BLOCK 3 and BLOCK 4). To end her solo, she plays a repeated rhythmic figure in octaves that Rashied Ali accentuates with his drums (indicated as BLOCK 5). Such readily identifiable rhythmic figures provide another stabilizing and punctuating element inside Alice's torrent of improvisation and give the drummer a clear signal to respond.

Released in 1995, Alice's work as a soloist on "Manifestation" was unfortunately unknown to the public. Her first major public debut with John Coltrane occurred with the recording *Live at the Village Vanguard Again!* in May 1966. (The title refers to one of Coltrane's most dissonantly expressive albums of his middle period, an earlier live recording that he had made with his Classic Quintet, with the addition of Eric Dolphy on reeds.) Alice did not perform any solos on this date—which is not unusual, given the focus on the two saxophonists, and the fact that in previous sessions, the pianist McCoy Tyner had played only accompaniment. Alice's playing on this recording demonstrates the same glissandi effects, dramatic pedal points, and colorful modality as in "Manifestation." These effects, however, now served the soloist.

The critical reaction to her playing on this record, particularly her interactive ability as an accompanist, was complimentary. In the album's liner notes, Nat Hentoff states: "Throughout, from the start of the album, there is the persistently apposite piano of Alice, John's wife. Her value to the group, Coltrane says, is that 'she continually senses the right colors, the right textures, of the sounds of the chords. And in addition, she's fleet. She has real facility'" (1961).

In a July 1966 tour in Japan, Alice had the opportunity to further develop her solo techniques before a live audience. The tour was an affirming experience for the band members. Having witnessed the mixed, often negative, reception of avant-garde jazz in America, they found Japan's hospitality and warm response a refreshing change. The drummer Rashied Ali explained: "When we came off the airplane they had life size posters of us . . . cut out to the shape of each one of us at the airport and then they took a red carpet and rolled a red carpet from the plane into the terminal for Coltrane. That's the way they did it in Japan" (quoted in Porter 1998, 272).

The six tracks released as *Live in Japan* were made on two concert dates in Tokyo, one at Shinjuku Kosei Nenkin Hall on July 11, and the second at Shankei Hall on July 22. On these two evenings, the band explored extremely long, free-form versions of Coltrane's earlier favorites—Mongo Santamaria's "Afro Blue" and Rogers and Hammerstein's "My Favorite Things"—as well as Coltrane's own compositions "Leo," "Peace on Earth," and "Crescent." Most of the tracks are at least thirty-five minutes long, which gives the soloists ample time to stretch out. In each of Alice's solos, one finds subtle references to the underlying compositions. In "Afro Blue," her preference for F minor and the extensive use of the F minor pentatonic scale summons back the original melody. Although she ventures to E-flat and E periodically to add color and tension, this improvisation remains solidly in F minor. Her solos on both "Leo" and "My Favorite Things" likewise remain in one tonal area, as in the original versions. By contrast, her improvisation on "Crescent" is structured by rapidly shifting tonal centers accentuated by left-hand pedal points. With the exception of "My Favorite Things," a tune characterized by its waltz time, none of Alice's solos has a defined beat or groove.

Perhaps her most beautiful improvisation on *Live in Japan* is that from "Peace on Earth." Here, Alice is left nearly alone by the rhythm section. With great liberty, she controls the color, range, and full dynamics of the piano. In this improvisation, we see a new musical identity emerge for her: that of concert pianist. Until this point in her recording career, the rhythm section and the needs of the soloist had driven her keyboard playing. She had not yet had the opportunity to make use of her classical training or demonstrate the subtlety of her technique. "Peace on Earth" showcases her command of the concert grand piano and displays the beginning of a more rhapsodic soloistic approach that she developed fully as a leader on her own projects. The chromatic alterations she uses on the subdominant chord (resulting in a variation of Lydian dominant) over a tonic pedal and the sumptuous swells we hear are reminiscent of the classical piano repertoire from late nineteenth and early twentieth centuries. However, the repeated movements from the tonic to subdominant that essentially define this improvisation are also thoroughly saturated with a feeling of the blues and the African American church. This synthesis of soulful gospel and classical technique characterize Alice's slow-tempo piano style in her husband's band. This combination would also find a mature expression in her more elaborate works for large ensembles.

In 1967, John Coltrane's health began to deteriorate—unknown to him, he was suffering from liver cancer—and he turned down invitations for several tours, preferring instead to document his ideas in the studio. With the exception of the newly released *The Olatunji Concert: The Last Live Recording,* in which Alice's playing is nearly imperceptible in the live mix, John Coltrane's last albums with his wife feature pared-down improvisations. On the albums *Expression* (recorded in February and March of 1967) and *Stellar Regions* (recorded in February 1967), Alice extracts the best aspects of her *Live in Japan* solos to color these dense musical miniatures. There is an intimacy and immediacy in the quiet dynamics and motivic instrumental conversations between husband and wife, which are made extremely poignant by the knowledge of John Coltrane's looming illness. Particularly moving are her accompaniment on "Jimmy's Mode" and the solos heard on "To Be," "Expression," "Seraphic Light," and "Tranesonic."

By May 1967, Coltrane was experiencing intense pain in his abdomen, and a biopsy revealed cancer of the liver. According to Alice, he knew his chances were limited on the operating table, and he declined to have surgery. By mid-July, he could no longer eat, and he checked himself into a nearby hospital. She recalled: "Maybe I didn't know how bad he felt because he wouldn't tell me. I used to leave him alone when I thought he wanted to be alone. I was busy with the kids and I didn't want to bother him, to get in his way, to bug him . . . He was such a strong man that he walked out the door himself. He was walking slow, but he made it. And then he went down so fast" (quoted in Garland 1969, 227–28). John Coltrane's death was an overwhelming loss for Alice and her family, not to mention the larger jazz community and the listening public. What we see in Alice's playing with John Coltrane's late Quintet is the "manifestation" of her unfettered creative self, made strong by the depth of her commitment to her family, her husband's musical vision, and a spiritual path of self-realization, which she would develop fully into her own deliberately mystical mix.

CHAPTER THREE

Universal Consciousness

Several years ago, following a long period of elementary meditating and reading of some of the diverse books on spirituality and world religions, I felt the deepest transcendental longing to realize the Supreme Lord. This longing within the depths of my heart was soon acknowledged, for within a short period of time I experienced the first rays of illumination and spiritual reawakening. On the physical plane these radiations opened new avenues of awareness in the brain cells; even subtler were the inner effects of light and the cognizance of a spiritual revelation taking place within me. —Alice Coltrane, *Monument Eternal*

After her husband's untimely death in 1967, Alice assumed the extraordinary task of carrying on John Coltrane's musical, spiritual, and familial legacy. She never rebelled against this responsibility or tried to differentiate her work from his. On the contrary, she wrote and performed a great deal of music in his memory and continually referred to him—often as "the Father" or by the spiritual name she gave him, Ohnedaruth (compassion)—as her primary musical mentor. She also maintained John's musical and spiritual philosophy and employed many of his creative strategies in her compositions. She even took up his signature practice of writing confessional, testimonial liner notes to accompany her music.

Because Alice made so little attempt to distinguish her music and her spiritual mission from those of her husband, particularly during her early years as a bandleader, she received many negative comments from members of the jazz establishment. For instance, John Litweiler's criticism of *A Monastic Trio* (1968), her debut album as a bandleader, was that it was too derivative of John Coltrane's musical concepts. Moreover, according to Litweiler, John Coltrane was not a musician whom one could or should emulate: "John Coltrane's music was so very personal, the emotion and lyricism so much a part of the man, the externals of his art so seductive and misleading, that no other modern musician is such a potentially wrong influence on other musicians. There have been other John Coltrane-influenced pianists before this, but on the evidence of 'Ohnedaruth,' Alice Coltrane is the first to assimilate his message almost completely into a personal style" (1969, 22).

While that statement has some validity, I would argue that as John Coltrane's devoted widow and spiritual partner, Alice was not concerned with artistic individuality—the sine qua non for critics' praise in modern jazz—but rather with honoring her husband's memory. And much to her credit, Alice actually made extremely constructive use of her husband's musical example: instead of copying John's improvisational lines or his phrasing style, as so many other artists did, Alice pursued his creative and spiritual ideology more broadly, ultimately inspiring her to produce extraordinarily innovative works.

As discussed in the previous chapter, John Coltrane's creative philosophy rests on three basic tenets—which Alice fully embraced—of music making based on personal expression: expressing an authentic self as a musician; erasing aesthetic boundaries and proscriptions regarding style; and branching out in an inclusive, pluralistic, and multicultural manner.

John Coltrane's creative ideology is manifested in Alice's preference for musical freedom and in her treatment of other musicians. Following her husband's example, Alice never returned to restrictive musical genres such as standards, bebop forms, or instrumental music with rigid tonal implications. She relied heavily instead on free meter, loose formal structures, and open-ended modality, and she encouraged timbral innovations from her instrumentalists. And like her husband, Alice created musical conditions in which her players could fully and spontaneously express themselves. For instance, when she conveyed her intentions to her band members, she did so in a nondictatorial, nondogmatic manner. Both jazz and classical players enjoyed and found uplifting the freedom and validation that she offered them. Her Impulse! producer, Ed Michel, explained her liberal approach in the recording studio:

> She would usually just play something. At that period, especially among the New York players, they thought of themselves as the free guys. That was where it was headed. You would suggest a harmonic environment, with a bass figure, and open it up from there . . . Especially in the beginning she would do that. She shared that desire to take whatever form existed and find a place where it would naturally, organically open up into what was a tremendously empowering space for musicians, who had the capacity to deal with it. It was an astonishing experience. A lot of the L.A. studio string players, who were symphony guys, when they first encountered it, thought, "wow, what's going on here?" and then ate it up. They loved it! (Telephone interview with author, 2001)

Along similar lines, even though Alice was on a decidedly spiritual path, she never made spirituality a requirement of her sidemen. As her former bassist Cecil McBee recalled, "She didn't say 'We're going to play spiritual, this is going to be something that is meaningful.' No, it was like, 'This is the way it feels. This is the way the bass line feels, and I'm going to play this.'" Yet McBee conceded:

> It was very, very spiritual. The lights were low and she had incense and there was not much conversation, dictation, or verbalization about what was to be. Her desire of your essence was all very, very tangible. The spiritual, emotional, physical statement of the environment, it was just there. You felt it and you just played it. It was very subtle but powerful. I can remember it to this day. It was all novel to me, but I knew that it was something very spiritual and very special. No doubt about it. (interview with author, 2001)

Throughout Alice's career as a bandleader, John Coltrane's "higher concept," as she termed it, did indeed emerge. Nevertheless—and much to her credit—her unique voice always came through. Continuing the exploration of free rhythm, rapidly shifting modality, and flexible formal structures that she began with her husband, Alice succeeded in bringing her own aesthetics to bear on her compositions, charting a musically bold and spiritually directed course of her own design. Alongside pieces for piano and small jazz combo reminiscent of her earlier work with her husband, her LPs as a leader consisted of ethereal meditations for harp, hard-hitting improvisations on Wurlitzer organ, and compositions for orchestra and choir based on *bhajans*—the Hindu devotional hymns. By the mid-1970s, Alice had clearly distinguished herself as a powerful and extraordinarily original voice in the jazz world who could recruit as her sidemen many jazz greats of the 1960s and 1970s, as well as orchestral players from New York and Los Angeles, and her students from the Vedantic Center.

To understand Alice's expanding compositional sensibility during years between 1968 and 1978, it is necessary to consider the nature of her spiritual transfiguration. Her work as a bandleader during this time can be divided into three periods that correspond to distinct stages in her artistic journey. While these periods are differentiated by her evolving musical aesthetics, they are also associated with progressive stages along her deepening spiritual path. During the first period, from 1968 to early 1970, Alice recorded *A Monastic Trio* (1968), *Huntington Ashram Monastery* (1969), and *Ptah the El Daoud* (1970). Except for her exploration of the concert harp as an improvisational vehicle, her music during this first phase is reminiscent of her collaborations with her late husband. In the second period, between late 1970 and 1971, she befriended the Indian guru Swami Satchidananda, recorded the album *Journey in Satchidananda* (1970), and traveled to India for the first time. Her liner notes during this period discuss the importance of her association with Swami Satchidananda and reveal a deepening interest in the religious philosophy of Vedanta, and in Indian music and culture. The third period, from late 1971 to 1978, is marked by extraordinary artistic individuation. Her works on the albums *Universal Consciousness* (1971), *World Galaxy* (1971), *Lord of Lords* (1972), *Eternity* (1975), *Transcendence* (1977), *Radha Krsna Nama Sankirtana* (1977), and *Transfiguration* (1978) feature powerful improvisations on the organ, compositions for orchestra, and arrangements of Hindu chants and hymns. This musico-spiritual phase reflects her own idiosyncratic religious synthesis and a newfound sense of creative omnipotence.

Tapas, 1968–70

This first phase of Alice's spiritual transformation coincided with the music she made shortly after John Coltrane's passing. From the time of her husband's death, she began to have extraordinary religious experiences. According to her description in her spiritual autobiography, *Monument Eternal*, the years 1968 to 1970 marked a period of spiritual purification for her, the first step on the path to spiritual enlightenment.[1] During this period, she experienced insomnia and an inability to eat or communicate for lengthy periods. She even injured herself in several of her "examinations" and was taken to the hospital on more than one occasion. Employing the term *tapas,* a yogic concept for spiritual austerity, she described her experience thus:

> My *tapas* in this lifetime initially began with increased waking hours and extended meditations. Long fasts were maintained and sleepless vigils endured. Extensive mental and physical austerities caused my body weight to fall from 128 to 105 within a few weeks; later it was reduced to 95 pounds. My physical *tapas* consisted of a series of examinations on my reactions and aversions, specifically to heat and cold, light and darkness, life and death, joy and sorrow—i.e., on the dualities of life-polarization. (A. Coltrane 1977, 17)

From a psychiatric perspective, it might appear that Alice was experiencing extreme depression or psychosis. Having recently lost both her husband and a half-brother to whom she had been close, and burdened with the responsibility of raising four small children, she would have had ample cause. However, she described this time as a necessary period of purification: "The mental and physical territories had to undergo purificatory spiritualization to bring about the expansion and heightening of my consciousness-awareness level . . . The Holy Spirit does not enjoy residing in an unclean heart" (ibid. 13, 24). While this period of extreme "spiritual suffering" took place during the years shortly following her husband's death, she described her *tapas* as an ongoing process that has "never ceased" (8).

The albums she recorded during this period, *A Monastic Trio*, *Hunting-*

ton Ashram Monastery, and *Ptah the El Daoud*, were extremely introspective and solemn. *A Monastic Trio* (1968)—her first solo album for Impulse!—was an intimate expression of personal loss and a tangible reminder of John Coltrane's musical and spiritual legacy. The liner notes also mark the beginning of her written communications with her audience, which would become increasingly extensive, mystical, and autobiographical.

The formal and improvisational techniques we hear on *A Monastic Trio* dominate her next two albums on Impulse! Recorded in the Coltrane Studio in Dix Hill, New York, with Rudy Gelder and Roy Musnug (her late husband's producer and technician) presiding, the album's session consisted of Alice Coltrane, on piano and harp, and John Coltrane's former sidemen: Jimmy Garrison on bass, Pharoah Sanders on saxophone and flute, and Ben Riley and Rashied Ali alternating on drums. Of the nine tracks on *A Monastic Trio*, eight are in minor modes, and five make use of rubato chord progressions that swell and ebb with a definitive weightiness. Alice also composed several elegies for her husband, among them "Ohnedaruth" and "I Want to See You." In the 1998 Cuscuna reissue of the album, the introduction to "The Sun" features the overdubbed voice of John Coltrane repeating the prayer "let there be peace and love and perfection throughout all creation, Oh God." Other titles suggest her struggle and transformation in the face of tragedy, such as "Lord Help Me to Be."

A Monastic Trio can be seen as the template for Alice's compositional sensibility at the start of her solo career. Nine original compositions are featured on the reissued CD, employing five distinct compositional devices. Three of these devices are clearly related to John Coltrane's musical tendencies, the first of these being the ostinato bass pattern that, while anchoring the composition tonally and metrically, demands adventurous risk taking on the part of the improviser. The solos that accompany these ostinato tunes result in modal mixture, expressionistic timbral exploration, and great rhythmic fancy. Such bass figures can be heard on the tracks "Lord Help Me to Be" and "Lovely Skyboat." The second compositional device is the rubato chord progression, which allows the soloist to remain in one tonal area as long as he or she likes; this device derives from John Coltrane's composition "Peace on Earth" and appears in Alice's compositions "The Sun," "I Want to See You," "Oceanic Beloved," and "Atomic Peace." The third device is akin to a mantra or prayer. Similar to the rubato chord progression, it is played in free time but comprises a simple theme played by two or more instruments in unison or octaves. John Coltrane popularized this technique in his later recordings *Ascension* (1965) and *Stellar Regions* (1967). We can see Alice employing this mantra technique in her composition "Ohnedaruth," in which the piano and bass share the theme.

While much of this work is derivative of her husband's music, Alice did succeed in making musical statements during this period that were unique to her. These include some compositional devices on *A Monastic Trio* that have not yet been discussed and that diverge from John's musical sensibility. The first is exemplified in "Gospel Trane," a pianistic blues-riffing tune that brings to mind Alice's training in the church. "Gospel Trane" is the only composition on the album to swing in a conventional sense. Eight-bar phrases, a rhythm break that sets up the blowing section, and a walking bass during the solo provide the compositional foundation. After the melody is stated, Alice departs from the rhythm section's steady pulse and embarks on her own free-form pianistic journey. A somewhat disjunctive return to the melody concludes the piece.

We see this blues piano aesthetic again in her two subsequent albums. For instance, her piano pieces "Jaya, Jaya, Rama," and "H.I.S." on her second Impulse! album, *Huntington Ashram Monastery* (1969), are similar piano blues features with free blowing sections. Additionally, "Turiya and Ramakrishna" and "Blue Nile" from her third Impulse! recording *Ptah the El Daoud* (1970), with sidemen Ben Riley, Ron Carter, Pharoah Sanders, and Joe Henderson, are straightforward twelve-bar minor blues tunes at moderate tempos. The first, "Turiya and Ramakrishna," is a gorgeous example of the piano blues tradition as it merges with a late-1960s modal aesthetic. Rather than journey into dissonance, her improvisation remains in E-flat minor and elaborates on the opening riff. Slow, pensive, and patiently articulated, this piano trio is one of the more moving and soulful statements of her early commercial recording career. Her superior capability here as a blues pianist speaks to both her upbringing in the church and the elegant blues influence that one can hear in so many great Detroit jazz pianists.

The final compositional technique on *A Monastic Trio* might be best described as a piano rhapsody; it can be heard on the solo piano track "Altruvista" and is similar in some respects to Alice's classically influenced work in her husband's ensemble. This piece, however, departs entirely from the theme-improvisation-theme structure that characterizes the majority of John Coltrane's tunes and, on a larger scale, jazz in general. Here, Alice's improvisational language departs from that of bebop, gospel, Coltrane, and jazz keyboard style, with its subservient left-hand voicings. "Altruvista" does not swing, nor does it rely on a blues-based melodic language. In its textures, modal exploration, and pianistic virtuosity, it resembles the piano compositions of Debussy and Ravel, though as an improvisation it is less formally structured than their music. In its timbre and use of range, it is reminiscent of Alice's solo on "Peace on Earth" from the *Live in Japan* recordings. Interestingly, although it is one of the loveliest and most original pieces on the album, "Altruvista" was not included on the first release, perhaps because it resembled twentieth-century art music as opposed to jazz. "Altruvista" is steeped in the intellectual and cultural sophistication of Detroit's black musical subculture, but also belongs to a realm of Alice's personal creative fancy. Most important, as an unaccompanied work, "Altruvista" hints of things to come: later in her career, Alice came to prefer the total independence of playing alone.

A Monastic Trio was not merely Alice's debut as a composer, it was also her debut as a multi-instrumentalist. The entire B side of the original LP features new compositions and improvisations for the harp ("Lovely Skyboat," "Oceanic Beloved," and "Atomic Peace"). The harp has never been a popular solo instrument in jazz; it has, however, been prevalent in new-age music, and Alice Coltrane has frequently been relegated to this musical category. The only individual to have achieved any prior success as a jazz harpist was another Detroiter, Dorothy Ashby, who had performed internationally with numerous Detroit jazz musicians, with some of whom Alice Coltrane had also played, such as the bassist Vishnu Wood. Like many of Detroit's famous jazz musicians, Ashby was trained at Cass Technical High School, which had an active harp and voice ensemble. Alice Coltrane's unusual confidence in the harp's potential was most likely grounded in her exposure to Ashby, as well as her past success as a multi-instrumentalist with Terry Gibbs. Her decision to play the harp was inspired by the interest that John Coltrane had shown in the instrument. In a radio interview in 1988, Alice stated: "Yes, that's why, he got me interested. He ordered that harp. I still have it today. His physical eyes never saw it. It took us a year to get it because they are practically handmade. He ordered a beautiful concert grand crowned harp. So he is really responsible for that being part of my life" (A. Coltrane 1988).

Self-taught on the instrument, Alice developed a unique style, relying extensively on pentatonic modality, glissandi, accented arpeggios, and pedal points. The harp offered Alice fresh sonorities and textures, and a new vehicle of expression. Speaking metaphorically of the harp's qualities, she said in an earlier interview: "The piano is the sunrise and the harp is the sunset . . . All that energy, light, brilliance, and clarity that's in the rising sun—or what we call rising; it's actually us moving over toward the light—you can hear in the piano. Then listen to the sonorities of the harp, the subtleties, the quietness, the peacefulness; that's like our sunsets. But the sun is always the sun and a person is always who he or she will be" (quoted in Lerner 1982, 27).

Many critics have erroneously attributed her florid piano playing to her training as a harp player. Alice's harp style, however, is best described as an extension of the technique she was already exploring at the keyboard. Critics have also dismissed her harp playing for its imprecise quality. In his review of *A Monastic Trio*, John Litweiler wrote that "the harp side of this LP presents waves of sound, a wispy impressionist feeling without urgent substance" (1969, 22). The harp does indeed present instrumental limitations and challenges; in particular, on that instrument Alice has far less ability to execute individual lines, an ability that has always been one of the hallmarks, if not requirements, of modern jazz. Unfortunately, Litweiler's assessment does not acknowledge the interactive and textural quality of Alice's playing, or the daring behind her search for new sonic environments. These early timbral and gestural explorations on the harp were the precursors of her later sound experimentations on a much larger scale.

Many critics and listeners who expected to find the volume and aggressive intensity that characterized her work with John Coltrane on her first three Impulse! recordings were disappointed. For instance, in his review of *Ptah the El Daoud*, Ed Cole stated: "It seems incredible that a group so heavily stamped by the late John Coltrane would not be able to pull off an album, but that's just what happens here. It's not that this is not good music, because it is, but it doesn't come close to the potential of the individual players. It seems that each subdued his talents to accommodate the others" (1971, 20). As a result, Alice Coltrane's music did not have the political implications that one could feel in the music of her avant-garde colleagues. Musicians such as the bassist Cecil McBee, however, who played for Alice, could see the subtle value of her quieter aesthetic and its relevance to the political climate of the era, compared to the excess of the avant-garde musical statements that were then popular:

> We were critical of the limits that were being placed on us. And we felt that our musical words could penetrate steel walls, so long as we said them with honesty, and perseverance, and creativity from the deepest [part] of ourselves. So we were political in that way. But things were rather novel, as far as civil rights were concerned. There were those who were much more eloquent than we were with words, like the Malcolm Xs and the Martin Luther Kings, the Angela Davises. We let them have that verbally, but we said it in music. And we were able to say it in music. We got across equally as well as they did with what we expressed. So Alice Coltrane, when she arrived, was more subtle in her statements, from a very spiritual point of view. She was very quiet, expressing the various sounds and waves of spirits and essences of the gods and the earth. Where we were trying to come from, with the loudness and bombast of our music, she made these statements in a more delicate, graceful, articulate, and uniform way than we did. (interview with author, 2001)

Although Alice Coltrane's commitment to her husband's creative ideology and avant-garde music would ultimately take her down extremely original musical paths, what we see in her first three records as leader—*A Monastic Trio*, *Huntington Ashram Monastery*, and *Ptah the El Daoud*—are still tunes that remain well within the fold of John Coltrane's compositional and improvisational aesthetic. These early LPs do not display the originality of her later work in the 1970s. Nonetheless, we do see a developing composer exploring new timbres and instrumentation, the relationship between structure and freedom, and the potential of quieter dynamics.

Self-Realization, 1970–71

According to the bassist Vishnu Wood, a musical colleague and fellow Detroiter, in 1969 Alice was still suffering emotionally in the wake of her husband's death. At the time, Wood was attending the lectures of Swami Satchidananda (1914–2002) on Manhattan's Upper West Side. Hoping that exposure to the swami's teachings would help to lift Alice from depression, Wood introduced them to one another. By early 1970, Alice had become a friend of Swami Satchidananda and regularly visited him to receive spiritual inspiration and guidance.[2]

It appears that her association with the swami was deeply healing. Emerging from her "spiritual austerities," she recorded *Journey in Satchidananda* in November 1970 and dedicated the album to her new guru; his poems, photos, and teachings adorn her subsequent Impulse! recordings. In her liner notes for *Journey in Satchidananda*, she wrote:

> Direct inspiration for *Journey in Satchidananda* comes from my meeting and association with someone who is near and dear to me. I am speaking of my own beloved spiritual preceptor, Swami Satchidananda. Swamiji is the first example I have seen in recent years of universal Love or God in action. He expresses an impersonal love, which encompasses thousands of people. Anyone listening to this selection should try to envision himself floating on an ocean of Satchidanandaji's love, which is literally carrying countless devotees across the vicissitudes and stormy blasts of life to the other shore. Satchidananda means knowledge, existence, bliss.

Journey in Satchidananda—Alice Coltrane's fourth album for Impulse!—expresses a new timbral and world-music aesthetic. This LP is an important transitional album between her first three Impulse! projects and her subsequent recordings, which reveal a more personalized aesthetic. With the exception of Cecil McBee on bass, the distinctive members of John Coltrane's former band—Rashied Ali and Pharoah Sanders—again grace the LP. But the sound of the ensemble is markedly different. For the first time, Alice used the tamboura, an Indian string instrument customarily tuned in fifths and octaves, to provide a hypnotic wash of harmonics. From then on, the droning reverberations of the tamboura would become a kind of musical signature for her, invoking the classical and folk music of South Asia as well as the spirituality that the West had come to associate with Indian musical traditions.

Journey in Satchidananda also features the oud playing of Vishnu Wood on the track "Isis and Osiris." The oud is a plucked lute associated with Arabic music from the Middle East and Northern Africa; Wood played it in an idiosyncratic style. Though the oud was not an instrument played in ancient Egypt, Alice uses it as an instrument to invoke Egyptian gods and goddesses, one of her many creative, yet inauthentic uses of world-music sources. "Isis and Osiris" is largely unmetered and features the bass playing of Charlie Haden, whom Alice would hire for several later dates. Although oud, harp, bass, drums, and soprano sax would never be played together in traditional settings, Alice combines them here, with beautiful textural results. These experimentations and juxtapositions of musical idioms characterize her future compositions.

Although the album was innovative in its textural conception, Alice relied on compositional devices from her first three Impulse! albums. For four of the five tracks on the album, she composed memorable bass ostinato patterns, over which she and Sanders play largely pentatonic improvisations. She also invoked the memory of her husband quite explicitly in the tune "Something about John Coltrane," a blues-inflected piano feature that expands into a free-meter improvisational section, allowing her band members ample time to stretch out. Although the influence of John Coltrane can still be heard on *Journey in Satchidananda*, the musical and spiritual culture of India clearly emerge here as a dominant influence in her music.

To understand how India became a spiritual and musical source that Alice regularly drew upon, one must look to her relationship with Swami Satchidananda. Although Alice had been reading Hindu spiritual literature before their encounter, it was the swami who introduced Alice firsthand to the religious and musical culture of South Asia. Following his example, she eventually became a swamini herself. The relationship that developed between them is of interest for the striking impact it had on her spiritual views, aesthetics, and future path. More generally, their friendship also demonstrates the influence of Indian spiritual traditions on African American musicians during the 1960s.

Perhaps because of the great degree to which Indian spiritual traditions have influenced America's elite white society, scholars have underplayed the extent to which the traditions have also influenced blacks in the United States. Hindu teachings—albeit in an exoticized form—have been part of mainstream American culture since the late nineteenth century, finding a particularly strong foothold in Northern intellectual circles. American interest in Indian spiritual traditions can be traced to the Transcendentalists, such as the influential thinkers Ralph Waldo Emerson and Henry David Thoreau, who mixed together elements from a variety of religious sources in their writings. In particular, Emerson, in his 1841 essays "The Oversoul" and "Spiritual Laws," popularized the Indian metaphysical beliefs that the world, God, and human beings all participated in one substance, and that beyond the illusion of matter lay the reality of the spirit.

Several decades after these essays were published, the Russian émigré Helena Blavatsky founded the Theosophical Society, whose primary mission was the study of comparative religions. Blavatsky invited Swami Vivekananda to speak at the World Parliament of Religions, an extension of the 1898 Chicago World's Fair. The first Hindu monk to lecture in the United States, Vivekananda's discourses on the philosophy of Vedanta, and the subsequent establishment of centers for Vedic study, inspired a generation of American intellectuals. In the 1920s, Paramahansa Yogananda, one of Vivekananda's brother monks, established the Self-Realization Fellowship in the United Staes. It remained the primary American center for the study of yoga until the 1960s.

There is some evidence to suggest that these concepts filtered into the spiritual philosophies of several black religions in Harlem during the 1930s. In *Mystics and Messiahs: Cults and New Religions in American History*, Philip Jenkins proposes links between the late-nineteenth-century "harmonial" movements of New Thought and Theosophy and black religious figures such as Father Divine and Sweet Daddy Grace. Jenkins also points to the highly eclectic and "metaphysical" orientation of such groups as the Church of the Living God and Negro Masonry (2000, 101).

A more direct African American cultural encounter with India occurred when the Reverend Howard Thurman and his wife, the musician and social historian Sue Thurman, led what they called a Christian Negro Delegation to India in 1935. There they met with Mahatma Gandhi and conversed at length about religion, colonialism, and racial issues in the United States. Howard Thurman's subsequent writings were greatly influenced by Gandhi's commitment to nonviolence. Thurman's work, in turn, influenced Martin Luther King Jr., who was said to have carried a copy of Thurman's 1949 *Jesus and the Disinherited* with him in his briefcase.[3] Sue Thurman went on to lecture about Indian civilization and raised funds in these lectures so that several African American women could study at the school of the Nobel Laureate Rabindranath Tagore, in West Bengal. In later years, Howard Thurman founded one of the first racially integrated churches in the United States, the Church for the Fellowship of All Peoples, in San Francisco.

In addition to these spiritual affiliations with India, African American radicals who sympathized with India's struggle for independence from British rule also forged more immediate political allegiances with India in the early part of the twentieth century. In *The Karma of Brown Folk*, Vijay Prashad notes that "the stamp of radical India was made popular in the black press" by such figures as W.E.B. Du Bois, who wrote: "the people of India, like American Negroes, are demanding today things, not in the least revolutionary, but things which every civilized white man has so long taken for granted, that he wishes to refuse to believe that there are people who are denied these rights" (quoted in Prashad 2000, 39).

In the early part of the twentieth century, the study of Indian religion also became a legitimate academic subject. Religious scholars of great intellectual ability—many of them Europeans, such as Mircea Eliade, Carl Jung, Gershom Scholem, and Henry Corbin—popularized the study of comparative religion in American universities. Their pursuits were bolstered by the work of structural anthropologists who explored myths and the principles by which they functioned to organize the societies of non-Western cultures. By midcentury, the study of Hinduism had become common on college campuses. Interest in India's classical music also emerged during this period, largely through the efforts of Yehudi Menuhin, a world-renowned violinist who promoted the the Indian virtuosos Ravi Shankar, Bismilah Khan, and Ali Akbar Khan, whose recordings were issued by Nonesuch Records. The so-called British rock invasion also put India and its musical and spiritual culture on the world map for Americans. George Harrison of the Beatles popularized the sitar and the teaching of his Indian guru, Mahesh Yogi, and other musicians and artists quickly followed suit. Besides John and Alice Coltrane, other well-known jazz artists whose study of Indian spiritual paths influenced or fused with their musical practice include Don Ellis, Paul Horn, and John McLaughlin.[4]

But despite the ways that India had infiltrated the American consciousness, Hinduism largely remained an exotic and occult religion in the United States. Unlike the Judaism, Islam, and Greek Orthodoxy practiced by immigrant groups, Hinduism in America remained an export religion until quite recently. It was not until well after the Asian Immigration Act of 1965 that South Asians became a significant presence in America, bringing their religion with them. In the wake of the 1965 law, several influential Hindu swamis arrived in the United States; they have largely been responsible for the present popularity of yoga in this country. Alice's guru was one of them.

When Swami Satchidananda arrived in the United States in 1967, he was fifty-three years old and a well-known spiritual teacher in his own country. For nearly two decades, he had studied and served under Swami Sivananda, whose writings Alice had read prior to meeting her guru. Swami Satchidananda had also traveled widely in India, establishing several branches of his master's Divine Life Society, an organization and network of retreat centers founded in 1936 that were committed to "a world-wide revival of spirituality through publication of books, pamphlets and magazines dealing scientifically with all the aspects of Yoga and Vedanta, universal religion and philosophy, and ancient medicine" (http://www.dlshq.org, accessed December 10, 2007).

At the invitation of writer and filmmaker Conrad Rooks, whom he met in 1966 in Ceylon, Swami Satchidananda came to New York, where he was the guest of the artist Peter Max. The swami attracted a group of American supporters and devotees, many of them artists and intellectuals, and quickly became something of a celebrity. He began lecturing weekly at the Unitarian Universalist Church on the Upper West Side and, soon after, founded the first Integral Yoga Institute at 500 West End Avenue. By 1968 his renown was such that he was interviewed by *Life* for its issue titled "The Year of the Guru," and his lecture at Carnegie Hall drew a full house. He also opened the 1969 Woodstock festival.

Swami Satchidananda's primary mission was the promotion of understanding among world religions and of selfless service to humanity. He felt that for worldwide peace to exist, individuals had to develop their capacity for unconditional love. To facilitate this, he developed the path of Integral Yoga, which encompassed leading a disciplined and balanced life; contributing to community projects; practicing meditation, *pranayama* (breathing techniques), and asanas (postures); and cultivating a personal relationship with the divine. He also assured his students that abiding happiness was a true possibility in their lives.

African Americans were a minority among Swami Satchidananda's devotees during the late 1960s, as they are today. Unlike other Eastern religions such as Nichiren Buddhism and Islam, which have large working-class and minority followings, Hinduism and yoga have generally attracted middle- and upper-class European Americans. Alice Coltrane's decision to explore Swami Satchidananda's teachings may reflect a certain middle-class consciousness on her part. However, her capacity to search for spiritual and philosophical knowledge in a predominantly European American context is testimony to her seeking spirit and her unwillingness to accept limitation and boundary, which had thus far propelled her through life as a professional musician. Furthermore, as an extraordinarily self-disciplined, independent, and inner-directed artist with a strong predilection for religious expression, Alice was uniquely suited to pursue the yogic and devotional lifestyle that the swami advocated.

By the late 1960s, it appears that Alice had also independently come to question the Christian teachings of her youth and found the Hindu belief in reincarnation sustaining. In 1971, she stated: "The Western Church has failed, especially with young people. It was set up to serve needs it's not meeting. Ask a Swami Hindu monk or someone else from the East about life after death and you'll get answers that are real about direct experience, about looking to God. It has helped me to go on" (1971, 42). More important, Alice found the concept of self-realization, an essential doctrine of Advaita Vedanta taught by Swami Satchidananda, deeply liberating.

Advaita Vedanta is a system of belief in which the self (the atman) is identical with the absolute (Brahman).[5] According to Vedanta, the absolute is without any attributes or qualities that can be specified or delimited. However, the absolute can be manifest in partial and lesser forms, such as a multitude of gods and images to which one might offer devotion. Although Advaita Vedanta allows for allegiance to many deities, liberation (*moksha*) is to be ultimately attained through knowledge of the self, which is also knowledge of the absolute. In an interview, Alice explained the appeal of this religious doctrine and how it differed from the institutionalized Christianity of her youth:

> The Eastern philosophy gives the aspirant the chance or opportunity to develop himself . . . Somehow the experience that I had, and I'm not going to speak for everybody, I'm speaking for myself . . . you go there and you hear the service and you get the instructions: prayer, to be faithful, trust, ask God's blessings. Yet, it never tells you what you can become—More Christ-like, more Christ-Conscious! There are certain wonderful statements made by Christ, "Greater works, shall ye also do," "I and my father are one." How is it that you can decide how this should be understood? If his word is the law then if he says, "Greater works shall ye also do" let me believe that! . . . He told you about your potentiality, your higher spirituality, but the church says get under that. Be less than [Christ]. I'm not stating we should be more than Christ, but you know, really. He says you have a higher, a greater potentiality. "I've fed five thousand. I want you to feed five million!" . . .
>
> To get self-realization. To get self-actualization, fulfillment. That's the point. And it isn't selfish—that term. It just means that you go to your fullest and highest potential, and not be limited by some tenants of some doctrine that says that we come here, here's the minister, and that we pay our tithes and go home and go back to your job or business or whatever and do everything you want. (A. Coltrane 1988)

In its inclusiveness and emphasis on personal potential, Vedanta is similar to the spiritual and creative philosophy that John Coltrane developed. It can also be seen as deeply rooted in the harmonial traditions of the nineteenth century, and in America's culture of authenticity. Interestingly, one also sees the language of self-realization in comments made by other experimental jazz musicians of the late 1960s and early 1970s. In his study of the Chicago-based black artists collective the AACM (the Association for the Advancement of Creative Musicians), George Lewis calls attention to the centrality of this concept among the collective's members. Lewis cites saxophonist Joseph Jarman in particular, who explained, "Up until the late sixties, we were always categorized, and it was only possible for you to self-realize certain situations. But then we began to realize that if you began to self-realize, you became a universal property, and then you must use the whole spectrum of conscious reality" (quoted in Lewis 2001–2, 110). Such comments lead one to believe that this spiritual doctrine was pervasive in the avant-garde jazz subculture, and not limited to Alice and the New York jazz scene.

Shortly after recording *Journey in Satchidananda*, Alice Coltrane joined her guru in India on the last leg of his world tour, making her first pilgrimage to holy sites in that country. As she mentioned in her liner notes to the album: "Bombay will be the first stop on my five-week stay in India beginning in December, 1970. I will be visiting New Delhi, Rishikesh, Madras, and the country of Ceylon"—thus the name of one track, "Stop over Bombay." According to Shanti Norris, who was Swami Satchidananda's personal assistant at the time, Alice's tour of India with the swami was quite intimate: "That particular trip was not a group trip. This was Swamiji traveling with one or two assistants. Those were the days when it was really informal and it was very wonderful. And though it was informal, the nature of their relationship was certainly teacher and student" (Norris 2003).

In New Delhi, Alice attended the World Scientific Yoga Conference, a meeting of gurus, scholars, and students. She spent several days in Sri Lanka (then Ceylon) at a spiritual retreat, journeyed to Rishikesh to visit the Ganges and Swami Sivananda's Divine Life Society, and spent time in Madras attending lectures and celebrations and visiting temples. Alice brought a harp with her to play at several public birthday celebrations for Swami Satchidananda. Norris recounted: "She literally bought a seat for it on several trips because we went from Delhi and then back to Madras and then to Ceylon or something like that. It was stunning to people there, that somebody came from the West to play, who's also African American, who brought this harp with her! Just imagine all that, and this is back thirty years ago. At that time, even any Westerner was greeted with great appreciation and interest and fascination. She made quite an impression—but she was always very modest" (ibid.).

On this trip with Swami Satchidananda, it is likely that Alice heard Indian classical and popular devotional music in its traditional context for the first time. Although the swami was not a musician himself, he encouraged and supported the arts and believed in music and chanting as a form of yoga. Norris explained: "I don't think I've ever been to India with him where I didn't go to chanting things, and Bharata Natyam, and classical music. Even though Swamiji wasn't so much of a musician himself, he was always an advocate and a supporter of the arts and the classical traditions, particularly those of South India" (ibid.). During the *satsangs*, or community gatherings, of the Integral Yoga Institute in its early days, members would practice *kirtan*: they would chant traditional mantras and sing Hindu devotional hymns as a form of *sadhana*, or spiritual practice. In Sanskrit, *kirtan* literally means "telling, repeating, or praising." As a musical term it is often used interchangeably with *bhajan*. In the most general sense, both refer to South Asian religious music in the form of an antiphonal song of praise or devotion to a deity.

Apparently, early in her studies with Swami Satchidananda, Alice Coltrane took to chanting. However, she added a quality of personal expression that moved Norris and has since moved many others:

> For me, she brought a kind of jazz element to traditional chanting. Whether or not that's actually true, for somebody who can analyze musical styles, I don't really know. But for me, I love really rocking out, devotional chanting. To this day she is one of my favorite all-time people. If I heard anywhere that she was leading a *kirtan*, then I would go in a second. Because she brought something different to that. There are places in India you can go where people really rock out and really chant, and still her chanting is different. It's that and some other element. Which is her, you know, uniquely her. Which is phenomenal, in my opinion. (ibid.)

After returning from India, Alice regularly arranged and adapted traditional Indian chants and hymns for various ensembles. The antiphonal, flexible, and improvisatory formal structures of Indian devotional music and its ecstatic nature are similar to those of both gospel and jazz music. Upon this aesthetic and sacred common ground—an enduring point of contact between African American and South Asian religious music—many of Alice's later hybrid musical concepts are based.

Universal Consciousness, 1971–78

In the liner notes to the album *Universal Consciousness* (1971), the first LP that Alice Coltrane (now known by her new spiritual name, Turiya) recorded after her trip to India, she emphasized the importance of her pilgrimage: "Having made the journey to the East, a most important part of my Sadhana (spiritual struggle) has been completed." Her trip to India—her "Journey in Satchidananda," if you will—had a dramatic impact on her spiritual evolution and her related aesthetic sensibility. After her return, her new creative goal went beyond that of making music in a technical or artistic sense: she was now determined to express "extraordinary transonic and atmospherical power," which could send forth "illuminating worlds of sounds into the ethers of this universe."[6] As evidenced on the last group of albums she made for Impulse! and Warner Brothers—*Universal Consciousness* (1971), *World Galaxy* (1971), *Lord of Lords* (1972), *Eternity* (1975); *Transcendence* (1977), *Radha Krsna Nama Sankirtana* (1977), and *Transfiguration* (1978)—the experience of her spiritual awakening could no longer be contained within the timbral palette of the jazz rhythm section, even at its most expressive and avant-garde. She began to explore the combined potential of the rhythm section, orchestral strings, tamboura, harp, piano, percussion, and her newfound improvisational vehicle, the electric organ.

The Wurlitzer organ, which she used for the first time on the album *Universal Consciousness*, allowed Alice to express a tremendous amount of emotional power and raw energy. Her decision to explore the organ was directly related to her interest in Indian music. In a 1971 interview, she stated: "If you go to India or other parts of the East, they'll use something like a harmonium, called a shruti box, to make a drone sound. The tambura also produces a drone that sounds on and on. That's organ!" (quoted in Lerner 1982 24–25).

The cutting sonority and the flexibility of the Wurlitzer organ allowed Alice both musical independence and the ability to permeate the dynamics of a large ensemble. This independence freed her to explore greater compositional and improvisational parameters. Unlike her choice of concert harp, which had been motivated by her husband's interest in the instrument, her decision to play the Wurlitzer came to her in a divine vision. She stated in an interview that she had originally purchased a Baldwin portable organ. She continued: "In one meditation it was told to me that the organ had reached an age where it wouldn't serve properly, and the precise instrument I should get was revealed to me. I could even read the insignia right there on the wood. So I went out to find the Wurlitzer I now have. I didn't need to do any research; it was just conveyed to me" (ibid., 24).

The Wurlizer, on which she would rely extensively, also gave Alice entry into the amplified sound of fusion and rock music that had come to dominate popular improvisational music, exemplified in her powerful playing with Carlos Santana in 1974 on their album *Illuminations*. However, it is highly doubtful that her decision to go electric was commercially motivated. Rather, it appears that as she emerged from the darkness of her spiritual battle, she needed to find a more complete instrument that could convey her newfound strength. She explained:

If the father [John Coltrane] had remained on this earthly plane . . . I'm sure I would have stayed with the piano, because it was very complementary to what he was doing. He had the power, intelligence, the skill, the knowledge to carry on. He didn't need anyone else so the piano served as a nice quiet complement, though it wasn't a necessity to his music. As I continued in my music after the Father left, I found other keyboard instruments a necessity, because I did not want to have to depend on anyone either. When I started playing organ—and it's the truth; I hope I'm not misunderstood—I found that I didn't need anyone! When you have two or three manuals and complete bass in the pedals, if you play it the right way, you don't need any percussion. Not that drums and bass aren't welcome. I appreciate the skills of people like Reggie Workman and Roy Haynes, those kind of people. They are very great musicians and contributors to music. But I tell you, when I began to play the organ, there came the freedom and understanding that I would never have to depend on anyone else musically. (ibid.)

True to her words, her organ improvisations can stand alone as testament to her newfound autonomy as an artist. With the possible exception of Sun Ra, no other avant-garde musician has explored the potential of the instrument to such an extent.

As Alice Coltrane committed herself fully to expressing her experience of the absolute, her compositional sensibility became increasingly daring. I believe the artistic originality that emerges in these albums was directly related to the ways in which her mystical experiences had been validated by her guru and her experiences in India. In trying to express the absolute—in the sense of Brahman as unbounded, all-encompassing, and inclusive—she was moved to reach beyond the musical boundaries of the jazz genre and fully explore other traditions and styles. She also came to rely on extremely personal communications with the Lord for inspiration and musical direction.

After 1971, Alice's commentary in her albums included elaborate descriptions of the stages that the soul passes through in its spiritual evolution, the nature of the outer galaxies of the universe, and conversations with God and his various musical and spiritual emissaries. These exegeses provide a particularly vivid window into her deepening mysticism and, like her music from this period, draw from an array of increasingly disparate sources. The liner notes for the second track on *Universal Consciousness*, "Battle of Armageddon," were the most extensive and syncretic of her recording career:

This Great spiritual battle takes place within the nethermost regions of the human soul, literally, every day. The conflagrations of the satanic forces of evil will wax strong until the day when the God-spirit within one's own heart deals the final death-blow which annihilates his enemy (ego), burns the raging flames of sins to ashes, and purifies one's lower nature.

Many manifestations assist the soul in this war. Beings like El Daoud, who is the chief Lord of Purgatory, and Swami Savananda will aid you. Mother Kali, The Universal Mother, will impart her Shakti (Energy). Jesus Christ will bear witness to the execution, Sri Ramakrishna will give to you the key that unlocks the secret chambers where funeral cake is served. Baha'u'llah will open up a well-spring of Life, from which flows the Divine Elixir.

Tao, the Great, who knows the Way, will bombard and destroy the whole regime of sea and air forces (abyssal and astral forces) of hate and enmity, while Hanuman, a master warrior during the days of the Ramayana, will lead regiments of heavily armored combat tanks, whose devastation so checkmates and demolishes all attacks by the foe that no army of demons (ill-will and evil) on this earth (terrestrial) can withstand its onslaught.

Ohnedaruth (John Coltrane), who since for years past repaired to a City of shining radiance, situated near a point in space where stands a mammoth Colossus of Three Worlds, will sound the valorous hymn to the dead in war, "Taps," on a flute (body), i.e., Tapas: austerity-ascetic discipline. After all unrighteousness, anger and sorrow have been crucified to death, Zoroaster, Moses, and Mohammed will gently remove your body (bondage) from the cross and carry it before the view of your mother and father, i.e., Mary and Joseph: Isis and Osiris. Isis then removes her veil (Isis unveiled, reveals the naked Truth, which includes initiation into the Mysteries), at the glorious sight of her son's Crucifixion. Tearless Mary: Isis, watches the Mummification (wrappings used to cover the most heinous crimes committed by everyone, and never a single iota or vestige of such acts may ever be divulged to anyone, Ad Infinitum, forevermore). The Vault-keeper lowers the sarcophagus down into the Mastaba Pit (where sins are entombed and eternally incarcerated and consumed into the fire of that great Crematorium), then secures the final bolt that locks the Crypt.

Sri Aurobindo, the all-informing source of the universe, whose center is omnidirectional, will maintain constant observation, and will keep fully open all Intrafractory Light (Rays or beams of astral light whereby masters and God-like beings freely traverse). Sphinx will encourage and protect you during your interment before Resurrection. Lord Buddha will never leave you. Then, after the final victory is won over death (loving things of the world, and not one's Maker), May the Creator, who is most high Bhagavan God and Lord, take His Seat, i.e., His Sita: wife (Bride, Christ, in marriage, Coronation) in your heart (His Home).

The above quotation is a potent example of Alice's use of multiple sources, which are unified and justified by what is for her the seamless and transcendent nature of the mystical experience. Though it is difficult to draw direct comparisons between her poetry and her music, her recorded tracks can be seen to demonstrate a similar aesthetic during this period. Starting with the album *Universal Consciousness*, Alice began to explore what she termed "a totality concept." In the liner notes for the title track on the album, she explained:

Universal Consciousness literally means Cosmic Consciousness, Self-Realization, and illumination. This music tells of some of the various diverse avenues and channels through which the soul must pass before it finally reaches that exalted state of

Absolute Consciousness. Once achieved, the soul becomes re-united with God and basks in the Sun of blissful union. At this point, The Creator bestows on the soul many of his Attributes, and names one a New Name. This experience and this music involve a Totality concept, which embraces cosmic thought as an emblem of Universal Sound.

On the album *Universal Consciousness* and, arguably, throughout the rest of her recording career, Alice expresses this "totality concept" by juxtaposing an array of musical identities that might not commonly appear together: contrasting instruments, a mix of composition and improvisation, and jazz, classical, and world-music sonorities.

Universal Consciousness is an example of both the breadth and array of compositional techniques found on Alice's recordings between 1971 and 1978. Two works on the album, "Battle of Armageddon" and "The Ankh of Amen Ra," are duets for drums and Wurlitzer. The music that depicts "Battle of Armageddon" is an avant-garde, up-tempo, free-meter duo. Resembling John Coltrane's composition "Leo," which also featured the mercurial drumming of Rashied Ali, the piece is a virtuosic romp for both players built on the repeated transposition and rhythmic variation of a single motif. An incessant and unrelenting movement forward characterizes the music. Here John Coltrane's influence is clearly part of the aesthetic. But with Alice's buzzing, warbling voice on the organ, she claims the tune as her own. "The Ankh of Amen Ra" is dedicated to her sister and includes a prayer to Amen-Ra, the ancient Egyptian god: "Amen-Ra bear us safe passage across the River Styx." The organ theme reverts to a comparatively conventional metered pentatonic melody, which Alice enhances with electronic effects and a driving, syncopated left-hand figure. Both are compelling, hard-hitting improvisations that defy the sexist criticism her first three albums received.

Alice also set the Wurlitzer in other, more complex environments, with a small string section, the harp, and a rhythm section. For these organ features, she composed innovative formal structures quite unlike typical jazz and blues forms. For the track "Universal Consciousness," she fused the sound of harp and strings and contrasted that sonority with the organ, producing an overall ABA free-meter form, with her up-tempo keyboard playing sandwiched in the middle. In an otherwise dissonant environment, several precomposed violin figures provide the organizational framework for the A section. The first is a tremulous motivic figure that gradually becomes longer and more complex. The second figure is a sustained unison that has the effect of neutralizing the previous agitation, and the third is a bold, angular motive. After the second figure is stated, the string parts separate, so that each of the four violin players (LeRoy Jenkins, Julius Brand, Joan Kalisch, and John Blair) explore different musical identities such as pizzicato, arco scrubbing effects in the middle and lower registers, harmonics, and free melodic improvisation. While the strings play, Alice complements the activity with unifying arpeggios on the harp. According to her liner notes, these three tracks each display the arduousness of spiritual purification.

Countering the fierceness of these tracks are three others—"Oh Allah," "Hare Krishna," and "Sita Rama"—that display the more blissful aspect of spiritual attainment after struggle: the sunshine after the storm. In the liner notes, Alice wrote: "Oh Allah" is a prayer for peace, unity and concord. The strings helped me to voice this plea, 'O Mustafa Lord Allah, bring forth us all together again. We can depend on You to envelop us in Your all-embracing arms of universal harmony, tranquility and love.'" The strings twice play an evocative, metered introduction at the top of their register. Then Alice establishes a pleasant E Dorian environment with the sweet and trembling organ melody that she played upon entering and the two planning chords, Em7 and F#m7, that support the organ solo. A conversation between strings and Wurlitzer ensues, backed by the rhythm section. The organ theme is, as Alice indicated, like a plea.

"Hare Krishna" and "Sita Rama" are the most strikingly original compositions on the album. Each is based on traditional Indian chants, which Alice described in the liner notes:

"Hare Krishna"
This mantra (chant) is known as one of the greatest and highest of all mantras. Within its structure can be found three of the most powerful names of God, i.e., Hare, Krishna, and Rama. These names are among the best and most beloved of God, and so dear to Him. Saints proclaim that the power of this mantra alone can confer illumination on anyone according to the degree of his faith. This music irrefutably transports my soul to one of the highest pavilions in creation. Near the spatial mansions of the Most High Paradise, I soar to the abode of the Exalted One, where up in the Gold Room, I lied down in perfect repose.

"Hare Krishna"
Hare Hare, Hare Rama, Hare Rama, Rama Rama
Hare Hare, Hare Krishna, Hare Krishna, Krishna Krishna

"Sita Rama"
This hymn is sung in nearly every home throughout India. It was the favorite of that great soul, Mahatma Gandhi. India is the birthplace of more than ten known incarnations of God. Sita is the wife of lord Rama. While in India, I saw mother Ganges River, and my father Himalayas, whose peaks are the highest in the world. "Om shanti."

The Upanishads say: "whoever utters 3½ crores (35 million) of times this Mantra composed of 16 names becomes freed at once from all sins. He is released from all bondages and gets Mukti (Liberation).

It is extremely difficult to trace the origins of *kirtan* and *bhajan* melodies in India. This poses an interesting challenge when it comes to analyzing Alice's works based on the genre. Set to texts by poet saints, these chants and hymns have been passed down orally for hundreds of years, and they have been changed and adapted to fit local styles. *Kirtan* wallahs, singers who specialize in leading devotional singing, have also composed new *bhajans* based on their own poetry. In the written collections of *kirtan* that have been assembled to facilitate group singing, it is extremely uncommon to find either written notation or authorship; one finds only text. This allows the musical experience to be flexible, evincing improvisation on the part of the song leader and ecstatic expression from the participants.

I have been unsuccessful in locating the specific tunes to which Alice is presumably referring. It may be that she has adapted the traditional melodies so much that they have become unrecognizable—or perhaps I simply have yet to find the source material. Nonetheless, the manner in which she appropriates these chants is fascinating. These adaptations of Indian devotional music are altogether different from those of the more widely known Western musicians who traveled to India in the 1960s to study devotional music. Figures such as George Harrison, or the currently popular Krishna Das, have kept the original source melodies intact, using them as the basis for folk-rock arrangements for European American group singing. By contrast, during her career as a bandleader, Alice saw the potential of *kirtan* as a transcendent, avant-garde vehicle for rhythm section and orchestra. Thus, rather than simply arrange the traditional hymns, she created a new devotional genre modeled as much on the participatory and functional aspects of the music as on the original melodic material. To the best of my knowledge, no other jazz or classical composer has used Indian devotional music in this fashion.

In Alice's adaptation of "Hare Krishna," the entire ensemble plays an opening rubato theme in unison, while Rashied Ali adds a patina of cymbals and bells. Similar to the Coltrane-influenced mantra device of her earlier recordings, this majestic orchestral effect became a standard, perhaps slightly overused, practice on her subsequent recordings. The opening melody appears to be an invocation and could very well match the text "Hare Hare, Hare Rama, Hare Rama, Rama Rama." The exact scansion, however, is difficult to determine. The organ enters, playing a theme in E major while the ensemble sustains a drone. The trills and curlicues of Alice's melodic line depart from the language of both jazz and classical music. They appear to be an approximation of *gamak*, or the ornamental figures that characterize Indian raga. The organ theme beckons an antiphonal response from the orchestra, and a second unison orchestral figure emerges. Gradually, Alice's organ solo emerges, embracing dissonance. This entire rubato form is then repeated, like a song with various strains in which the verses comprise a free-jazz environment for organ and rhythm section.

"Sita Rama," her second *kirtan* arrangement, is perhaps the most Indian of her tunes thus far considered. The strings are absent here, and the tamboura and drums begin by establishing the drone. Another slowly expanding organ improvisation emerges resembling *alap*, the unmetered melodic exposition of raga in classical Indian music. This is followed by a more clearly defined melody that becomes the basis of improvisation. This structure is quite typical of Indian improvisational music. However, the entire conception is literally jazzed up with the sound of the rhythm section and overdubbed harp arpeggios. After this sonic environment has been established, Alice closes with an entirely new ethereal musical moment, using only harp and percussion.

Universal Consciousness is among the best of Alice's commercial recordings. Her string arrangements are highly inventive, resembling neither the settings nor the background figures of mainstream jazz standards. Nor do they resemble the high modern works of Gunther Schuller's third-stream projects or the idiosyncratic arrangements of other avant-garde composers, such as Ornette Coleman. Alice's semicomposed, semi-improvised compositional structures are also unique. The overall freshness of her approach, the combination of musical elements, her own daring Wurlitzer improvisations, the tremendous work of her sidemen, and the general balance and contrast of compositions are stunning. Nonetheless, despite the positive reviews it received in *Down Beat*, the album is little known among jazz aficionados, even fans of avant-garde jazz. Hybrid in its conception and situated between her derivative early albums and her more heavy-handed orchestral projects, *Universal Consciousness* has not received adequate praise or recognition.

Alice's two remaining albums for Impulse!—*World Galaxy* (1971) and *Lord of Lords* (1972)—are similar in their "totality concept" to *Universal Consciousness.* Here, however, Alice explores the potential of a full orchestral string section with varying results. On *World Galaxy* she arranged her late husband's signature tunes "My Favorite Things" and "A Love Supreme" with all the strings playing the well-known thematic material in unison. Voiced in such a fashion, the original compositions lose the trance-like quality that made them originally so appealing. She also wrote several works for *Lord of Lords* based on long, unison, blues-based melodies for strings, specifically "Andromeda's Suffering," "Sri Rama Onhedaruth," and "Lord of Lords." Although she contrasts these homophonous pentatonic invocations with exciting moments of dissonant, free improvisation, there often seems to be no middle ground. Successful in small jazz ensembles, this mantra technique is a rather heavy-handed device for a full string section. Absent on these orchestral tracks is the spontaneity and contrapuntal interest of her scaled-down string arrangements on *Universal Consciousness.*

It seems that Alice was aware of her shortcomings as an orchestral composer and welcomed the opportunity to develop her techniques further. As many classical composers have done, she chose to explore and arrange the works of symphonic masters. On *Lord of Lords,* she adapted excerpts of Stravinsky's *Firebird* Suite and the famous "Largo" of Dvorak's *New World* Symphony. Her choice to tailor these compositions rather than those of other nineteenth- or twentieth-century composers is rather compelling from a musicological standpoint. Both Stravinsky and Dvorak drew heavily on European folk melodies and successfully incorporated ethnic traditions into an art-music aesthetic. Perhaps on some level, Alice was attracted to the boundary-crossing dimensions of their work, which was similar to her own. Of course, Stravinsky's polytonal explorations, mastery of timbre and orchestration, and genius in disguising and displacing meter, were of particular interest to jazz modernists such as Charlie Parker and Miles Davis as early as the 1940s.

In her adaptations of both Stravinsky's and Dvorak's work, Alice boldly proceeded to absorb their compositions into her own aesthetic framework. From Stravinsky's *Firebird*, Alice adapted material from the "Introduction" and the "Final Hymn," the most lyrical of the suite's eleven movements. In the written portions of her arrangement, she kept quite close to the score. However, in the absence of woodwinds in her own ensemble, she plays their themes on the organ. In fact, she arranged nearly all of the melodic interest and solo excerpts for herself. At the end of the "Introduction," she inserted an interlude for improvising organ, backed with partially improvised and partially notated string figures. From these emerge the theme from the final movement, which is also played on the organ. Here she diverged only slightly from the formal aspect of the score in the "Final Hymn." In the final coda, however, she allowed for freely improvised textures.

Given Stravinsky's appropriative tendencies as a composer, there is a wonderful irony in the manner in which Alice has molded portions of *Firebird* into a free-jazz improvisation and made her voice on the organ central to the work. This is an act of daring requiring an enormous sense of creative license. As a mystic composer, Alice was conveniently relieved of the full burden that attends such artistic risk taking. In her liner notes to "Excerpt of Firebird," she wrote:

> On March 20, 1972, I was blessed with the good fortune of receiving a visitation from the great master composer, Mr. Igor Stravinsky, whom I had never met before in life. After a warm and intimate discussion on the subject of music, he said: "I want you to receive my vote." I did not fully understand his meaning. He then presented me with a small glass vial containing a clear, colorless liquid. He was seated in a

comfortable armchair; he held me close and said, "Daughter, this vial was for your grandmother, but instead, I kept it in reserve for you." He then asked if I would like the elixir, I said yes. As he walked away for it, I began to drink from the vial. To my surprise it was difficult to swallow. When it was finished, Mr. Stravinsky returned. Since that time, I have kept the album photograph from Mr. Stravinsky's *Rite of Spring* in my room. As opposed to this photograph, he had the appearance of an elderly man, but none of the weariness or age lines shown on his face.

Since that time, it has been incumbent on me to proceed forthrightly into the great master Stravinsky's works. Divine instruction has been given me throughout the entire arranging of this music, even down to the smallest detail. Ohnedaruth, when he was John Coltrane, seven years ago, introduced to me the music of, as he termed it, "a Universal musician and composer," Mr. Igor Stravinsky.

Clearly Alice derived enormous authority from her personal communications with the divine. Additionally, and perhaps more importantly, the divine could manifest through various emissaries or gurus for her: even a figure such as Stravinsky could be seen as a messenger of musical wisdom. In her mystical orientation, then, an enormously wide-ranging set of musical influences could be spiritualized and absorbed into her aesthetic.

"Going Home," Alice's setting of Dvorak's "Largo," is equally fascinating, particularly for the manner in which she has reappropriated the African American musical sources that the composer originally borrowed. Written in 1893, Dvorak's Symphony No. 5 in E minor hails from his American period, when the Czech composer was living in the United States and incorporating themes from black American and Native American sources in his own compositions.[7] The theme of the "Largo" was most likely modeled after the spirituals that Dvorak's black American composition student Harry Burleigh had sung for him. It may also have been based on selections from a vocal collection called *Negro Music* that had been in Dvorak's possession (Beckerman 2003, 132).

In 1922, roughly thirty years after the debut of the *New World* Symphony, William Arms Fisher, another of Dvorak's former students, set the "Largo" as a song and titled it "Going Home." "Going Home" soon became a popular gospel hymn and several decades later became a jazz standard:

Goin' home, goin' home, I'm a-goin' home;
Quiet like, some still day, I jes' goin' home.
It's not far, jes' close by, through an open door,
Work all done, care laid by, gwine to fear no more.
Mother's there, spectin' me, Father's waitin' too,
Lots o' folks gather'd there, all the friends I knew,
All the friends I knew. Home, home, I'm goin' home.

Rather than playing "Going Home" as a gospel arrangement, Alice maintained the symphonic aspects of Dvorak's "Largo." She copied his string

Fig. 3.1 The A theme of Dvorak's "Largo."

Fig 3.2 Coltrane's interpretation of Dvorak's "Largo."

orchestration, chord voicings, and many of the formal aspects of the original. However, she reclaimed the work by adding a solo harp introduction based on the movement's second theme and inserting an organ solo where the development section belongs. Strikingly, she also varied the movement's thematic material. She arranged the original English horn passages, which carry the melody, for the organ. In her highly personal treatment of the melody, she used the language of the blues and her gospel-inflected jazz touch at the keyboard. Compare the two following versions of the melody below. The first (figure 3.1) is a simple reduction of the A theme of the "Largo" and the second (figure 3.2) is Alice's interpretation of the same material:

Notice how Alice expands the melody by extending and elaborating two-beat phrases. Notice also the extensive use of pick-up notes, blues inflection, and the freedom of ornamentation in her version, all of which can be seen to constitute an African American singing and playing style. Though Dvorak based his "Largo" on black American musical sources, he captured none of this spontaneity and rubato phrasing style in his symphonic arrangement. I see Alice's variation of this theme as an African American reclamation of the melody.

In the liner notes for "Going Home," Alice reflected on the enduring value of African American spiritual music. She also appeared to contemplate her own relationship to the religious traditions of her youth and her connection to an African American past:

> Going Home is a gospel-oriented spiritual that is sung in homes and churches throughout the United States today. It was one of my parents' favorite songs. Gospel and Spiritual music are some of the greatest Attributes of the Creator to have been bestowed abundantly upon the children of the Nile, i.e., African Americans.
>
> A classical composer, Anton Dvorak, heard this music and built it into a concert piece within the context of his "New World Symphony." He titled it "Largo."

> One day I asked the Lord about coming Home at the end of my life. The Lord said to me, "Turiya, you will not have to come home, you will Be Home." Be and Being are some of the Absolute aspects of the Creator. Man tries, he hopes and struggles, he searches and dreams, he gets confused; but not so with the Almighty Infinite Lord. There is not a modicum of strife or struggle, no hopes or expectations, no trials or errors or fears. A soul who can Be one with the Lord will discover that his true identity is that of a God-like being, resembling in likeness and appearance, and expressing in the creativity the majesty and Perfection of his creator.

In questioning the Lord about "coming home," her commentary suggests a certain ambivalence regarding her own musical and spiritual path. By the end of the passage, however, Alice has found strength and sustenance once more, in a simultaneously personal and transcendent experience of the divine.

Lord of Lords was the last album that Alice Coltrane made for the Impulse! label. In the three years before *Eternity*, her next commercial release with Warner Brothers in 1975, a series of great changes again took place in her life. She moved to California, settling first in the Bay Area and then in Woodland Hills, near Los Angeles, where she lived the rest of her life. More important, she obeyed the call to renounce the secular life and become a monastic. Between 1972 and 1975, her time was increasingly spent ministering to a burgeoning group of religious aspirants who sought her teachings and wisdom. Gradually her life as a professional musician gave way to her life as a guru. She did, however, make two albums as a side person before 1975, first playing harp for Joe Henderson on *The Elements* in 1973, and then writing string arrangements and playing harp and Wurlitzer organ for Carlos Santana on their album *Illuminations* in 1974.

In the early seventies, A.B.C and Impulse! were undergoing large administrative changes. Ed Michel, Alice's Impulse! producer, followed her when she made the move to Warner Brothers. He explained: "A lot of artists got dropped, a lot of contracts expired and weren't renewed. Various people had been poaching for Alice, because they knew her contract was coming to an end. Bob Krazner signed her at one point, and I think he was instrumental. He wanted to sign four artists from Impulse! and move them over to Warner. Alice was the only one that went" (telephone interview with author, 2001). Needless to say, Alice's artistic persona during this period was quite eccentric. Michel put that in context:

> Some people thought she was really weird and far out. Some people thought Richard Nixon was really far out! . . . Remember, the late '60s to mid-70s was the most open period in American commercial music and radio. Astonishing things were being broadcast. Everybody could record and put things out and it was a wonderful time for the music. There was an openness. Distributors, who were often the bottleneck, were much more willing to take things on. (ibid.)

Despite the comparative flexibility of the recording industry, Alice's "totality concept" posed a problem for Warner Brothers. The music that Alice produced was not what the label had expected. In this late period of her commercial career, her albums tended to lack a unifying musical concept. For instance, *Eternity* (1975), Alice Coltrane's first Warner Brothers release, featured a miscellaneous array of experiments, some reflecting her prior work on Impulse! and some altogether new. The first track, "Spiritual Eternal," is a 12/8 blues for organ and orchestra with a studio horn section. Aside from her mildly dissonant organ improvisation, this track—with its trumpet and sax choir, catchy theme, and swinging rhythm section—might well fall within the genre of rhythm and blues. "Wisdom Eye" follows, a koto-like solo piece for harp whose only connection to the prior track is the use of minor pentatonic. The third track, "Los Caballos," diverges yet again in its aesthetics. Here Alice attempts to convey her new love of horses in a rhythm-section tune featuring Charlie Haden on bass and several Latino musicians on timbales and hand percussion. The remaining tracks are equally contrasting. "Morning Worship" is a free-form jazz improvisation for organ, bass, drums, tamboura, and wind chimes, dedicated to the goddess Kali. "Spring Rounds" is an orchestral adaptation of Stravinsky's *Rite of Spring*, similar in conception to her setting of *Firebird*. "Om Supreme" is her first recorded track with a choir.

With such a wide and unconventional array of material on her first three Warner Brothers albums, it is no wonder that the label was somewhat concerned. It is generally difficult to find listeners with such eclectic tastes. As Michel explained, "Warner Brothers wasn't really crazy about it. They were much 'pop-ier.' They knew Alice was selling and wondered why she was doing something different. I would get calls from various people, 'Hey why don't you do this? Why don't you do that?' And, of course, I would reply, 'Why don't you do this and why don't you do that and leave me alone! Leave my artist alone! You signed my artist—trust my artist. If you don't like my artist, someone else will sign my artist!'" (ibid.).

With respect to the trajectory of her career, "Om Supreme" is perhaps the most important track on *Eternity*. Here Alice composed a vocal work that drew from *bhajans*. Combining English and Sanskrit phrases, she wrote her own lyrics, which described the different *lokas,* or planes of existence, in the Hindu cosmology. "Om Supreme" forecasts her future adaptations of *kirtan* with her students at the Vedantic Center at Sai Anantam Ashram in the choir; however, it lacks the ecstatic quality that her devotees would bring to her later adaptations of *bhajans*. Following the suggestion of Ed Michel, Alice hired professional singers for the session, European Americans who sang in an extremely restrained, enunciated style typical of the Cambridge

Singers. Though the choir is quite good, its lack of freedom and blues inflection sound awkward next to Alice's Fender Rhodes piano. A huge stylistic disjuncture occurs when the choir enters after a lengthy gospel introduction at the keyboard. This was the only time she used classical singers in her vocal arrangements. After "Om Supreme," she relied on the voices of her students, the majority of whom were African American men and women with gospel and blues-based musical backgrounds. On her next two Warner Brothers albums, *Transcendence* (1977) and *Radha Krsna Nama Sankirtana* (1977), she recorded two sides of traditional *kirtan* for her choir and the Fender Rhodes. These works will be discussed at length in the concluding chapter, as they are the forebears of the *bhajan* ritual that structures spiritual life at her ashram in Agoura Hills.

Alice came to rely almost exclusively on her vocal adaptations of traditional *bhajans* in her Avatar recordings of the 1980s and 1990s. But she remained committed to and supportive of instrumental avant-garde music. In fact, the last commercial recording she made before her long hiatus from public performance was not a *kirtan* album, but a hard-hitting trio project that evoked both her playing with John Coltrane and the avant-garde music of her earlier years. *Transfiguration* (1978), her farewell to the jazz business, was a live album featuring Roy Haynes on drums, Reggie Workman on bass, and a small string section. Despite her return to this jazz template, the spiritual intent of the music was central to the project. The liner notes to the title track explained that "'transfiguration' transforms every musical statement in this piece from a mere expression of one's mental prowess and musical capabilities into an offering of love and devotion in adoration and glorification of God, the Supreme Lord."

Of the five tracks on the album, two are piano features and three are driving, free improvisations for organ and rhythm section. The first piano feature, "One for the Father," is a memorial to her husband reminiscent of her playing on *A Monastic Trio*; it is a solo rhapsody built on a rubato blues progression and minor pentatonic elaborations that displays her command of the concert grand piano. The second is a composition for piano and strings entitled "Prema," based on the minor pentatonic melody of "Om Supreme." "Transfiguration" and "Affinity" are her own tunes based on pentatonic modality, and "Leo" is a spectacular trio version of her husband's famous composition.

Her introduction to "Leo," entitled "Krishnaya," is perhaps the most touching moment on *Transfiguration*, a moment that displays both where she has been and where she is headed musically and spiritually. Sitting at her organ in front of a large live audience in her orange robes, she plays a lovely plagal progression over which she thanks her sidemen and introduces her husband's piece. For a quiet moment, before unleashing a tremendous force of creative energy, she "has church," in the concert hall. As "Leo" ensues, she plays in a furiously motivic fashion reminiscent of her husband's late improvisatory style. Her up-tempo keyboard work here is the most exciting of her commercial career. With its rapid-fire transpositions of short figures; its long modal passages, rhythmic play, and timbral inventiveness; its sustained energy and burning pace; and the unrelenting support of Roy Haynes and Reggie Workman, she takes leave of the jazz business with a truly breathtaking swan song.

CHAPTER FOUR

Glorious Chants

Bhajan chanting extols the magnificence and the holiness of God. It celebrates the divine glories of the Lord. Chanting consists of worshipping God through song and music . . . Chanting removes agitations or vrittis from the mind, and brings peace. It edifies one, uplifts the spirit, purifies the atmosphere, and elevates the consciousness. —Alice Coltrane, *Mantra*

In 1976, Alice Coltrane had a revelation in which she received divine instruction to renounce secular life and don the orange robes of a swami, or spiritual teacher in the Hindu tradition. Thereafter, she was known as Swamini (the feminine form of "swami") Turiyasangitananda; she translated her "anointed" name from Sanskrit as "the Transcendental Lord's highest song of bliss." Typically, a Hindu monk or guru ordains a swami into a recognized lineage; however, according to Alice, her initiation came directly from the Lord, resembling the call to preach in her family's Baptist faith. In the last interview she granted before passing away, Alice recalled her experience:

It started with taking sanyas. That was a total mystical experience. It was God's deliverance of his anointed mercy on me. I was told the night and time, and to be prepared, so I got ready and put on a white dress and all, and I noticed when the time came, the colors of orange were poured into the cloth of the dress I was wearing. And I just watched it happen. I just watched everything go into that beautiful saffron color. And my name was given, of course, and the whole outline of the duty, the work and mission were also revealed.

One of the directives given to me was to start the Ashram . . . At first, I don't think my idea was on sanyas (renunciation) as much as it was on having the availability to seek the Lord, to be able to study spiritual scriptures and just to really immerse myself in living the spiritual life as much as possible. My children, I had raised them, my husband had passed some years ago. I had reached a point where most of my duties as a householder were fulfilled. It gave me the time to want to see, to want to strive, to want to devote quality time, because, you know the work of a woman is so full! I mean it's sometimes twenty-four hours. So once that was reduced, I had additional time that I could apply to the path, and that's what I've been doing. (A. Coltrane 2006, 36–38)

Alice's liberty from her "duties as a householder" and her freedom from an established religion allowed her the opportunity to develop a sui generis spiritual practice. As part of this pursuit, she began composing and adapting *bhajans* (Hindu devotional hymns) for the handful of spiritual followers that she had attracted in San Francisco during the early 1970s. Today, these hymns form the basis of musical worship services at Sai Anantam Ashram, the alternative spiritual community that Alice established in 1983. They are sung twice a day during the week, and once a day on the weekends.

In total, Alice made five studio recordings of these *bhajans,* the majority of which are noncommercial and fairly difficult to obtain. The earliest can be found on the B sides of *Transcendence* (1977) and *Radha Krsna Nama Sankirtana* (1977), both on the Warner Brothers label. Alice's arrangements of "Sivaya," "Ghana Nila," "Bhaja Govindam," "Sri Nrsimha," "Govinda Jai Jai," "Ganesha," "Prema Muditha," and "Hare Krishna" on these albums feature her choir and her lively accompaniment on her Fender Rhodes piano. In her liner notes, she thanked her students at the Vedantic Center "who have lifted their voices and hand percussion in praise and adoration of the Supreme Lord." The remainder of her *bhajans* can be heard on *Divine Songs* (1987), *Infinite Chants* (1991), and *Glorious Chants* (1995), all released on Avatar Book Institute, an independent label affiliated with the Vedantic Center. They feature Alice on keyboard, her choir, and a small string section, processed evocatively with studio effects and overdubbing. With the addition of *Turiya Sings* (1982), a solo album recorded in a marathon fifteen-hour session in which Alice chanted Hindu mantras by herself, these Avatar releases were the only recordings she made after leaving the commercial music industry in 1978, until she resurfaced with her final jazz album, *Translinear Light*, in 2003.

Quite remarkably, at Sai Anantam Ashram, Alice's *bhajans* have come to function as part of the religious ritual. According to the religion scholar Catherine Albanese, religious rituals "act out the insights and understandings" in a given belief system; they "serve to bring the community together"; and they "structure the daily lives" of members (1999, 10). Alice's *bhajans* perform all of these tasks for ashram members, but what makes the hymns unique is that they enact her singular spiritual philosophy. To gain a nuanced appreciation of the hymns—their organic evolution, their hybrid devotional aesthetics, and the ritual function they serve—it is best to view them in the context of a community that has revered Alice as a guru and has followed her teachings. First, however, one must have some idea of the nature of her belief system.

Creed

While it is beyond the scope of this book—and perhaps beyond anybody's capabilities—to systematize Alice Coltrane's unique spiritual philosophy, a core set of beliefs permeates both her ashram's website and the spiritual treatises that she wrote during her monastic period: *Monument Eternal* (1977), *Endless Wisdom I* (1981), *Divine Revelations* (1995), and *Endless Wisdom II* (1999). Chief among these beliefs are the notions that the soul of each individual is divine; that enlightenment, or "God-realization," is a possibility here on earth; that establishing a personal, devotional, and unmediated relationship with the Lord is a prerequisite for spiritual advancement; and last, that God does not belong to any one religion. Within this spiritual framework, Alice acted as "an instrument of the lord" and produced pages of "direct writing" and divinely inspired music that functioned as "free-telling" vehicles of transcendence, to borrow from William Andrews (1986a, 290). And quite remarkably, she integrated these beliefs into a lived religion and a devotional music practice at her ashram.

Alice was a spiritual maverick with respect to her Protestant upbringing. One sees this most clearly in the Hindu concepts that pervade her writings and teachings. Nevertheless, crucial aspects of her faith remain consistent with that of her evangelical sisters, past and present. Alice believed that "the essence of eternal bliss and happiness is within him, in the human heart—the earthly home of the soul, one's own true self" (1981, 22). This unshakeable belief in the soul's inherent divinity is consistent with the spiritual views maintained by eighteenth- and nineteenth-century black female preachers. As opposed to a theology that focused on "the casting off of sin," black female preachers have been primarily concerned with "reclaiming . . . an original blessing" (Connor 1991, 4). Typically, this "sacralization of identity" comes about through a process of conversion and the sublimation of personal identity. As Jean Humez writes, "in an apparent paradox familiar in religious thought this denial of her individual self enabled her to make the strongest possible assertion of the power and reality of her inner strength and knowledge" (1981, 2).

This denial of self and assertion of divinity has also allowed female preachers to maintain their private lives while fulfilling extremely public roles. In her study *From Sin to Salvation: Stories of Women's Conversions, 1800 to the Present*, Virginia Brereton explains that "one advantage of the absence of individual voice or of interest in personal circumstances was that converts could speak or write publicly of their deepest, most shattering moments, without really giving up their privacy" (1991, 18). Alice similarly surrendered attachment to her worldly and individual identity in order to serve God.

Ultimately, and paradoxically, this allowed her to maintain her private life and that of her family, while remaining in the spotlight. In her last interview, she stated,

> After a while you just aren't involved in the personality. God teaches us to be selfless and egoless, so you aren't involved with personal distinctions. You are really about the work, service, duties, and my concentration is on that greatly. We have to be selfless in our service so we can truly dedicate our life to our work, spend our lives seeking the Lord and living in obedience to the will of the Lord. Devotion and selflessness are such requirements. Because if we are self-interested or involved with our own importance, our own aim, we cannot serve the Lord that way. (A. Coltrane 2006, 37)

While Alice fervently preached that the soul was divine, she also maintained that realizing of one's divinity was a possibility here on earth, arguing that "perfection and freedom can be experienced not only in the heaven worlds, outside or around this universe, but right here on earth" (1977 36). She described this state as "Absolute Consciousness" or "Self-Realization," which "affords a kind of freedom in which the soul lives and moves around like a sovereign of this universe" (27). Belief in the possibility of enlightenment in this lifetime distinguishes her spiritual views from those of evangelical Christian women, whose eschatology has traditionally offered only "the promise of a rich and glorious afterlife" (Haywood 2003, 23). However, Alice's zeal to testify to the existence of heaven was equally passionate. For her, "liberation from the bondage of the external world" should be the very goal of life (1981, 23). In part because she herself claimed to have experienced this state, there is urgency and passion in her writing and musical expression. It is as if everything she did asked the question: "why would anybody want anything else if this is a possibility?"

Nevertheless, Alice found the journey to self-realization a demanding one that required great self-discipline, effort, and introspection. To achieve this state of "Absolute Consciousness," one must purify one's mind and actions. Alice also claimed to have experienced this arduous process. In fact, the most dramatic aspect of her spiritual autobiography is the description of *tapas,* or self-imposed austerities, that she endured between 1968 and 1970: "my physical *tapas* consisted of a series of examinations on my reactions and aversions, specifically to heat and cold, light and darkness, life and death, joy and sorrow—i.e., on the dualities of life-polarization" (1977, 17). She also described extreme "mental tests" that included enduring deafening sounds, extreme vibrations, disorienting "out of body" experiences, and bewildering encounters with spirits (ibid., 19). The benefits of Alice's self-imposed austerities were "spiritual perceptions . . . bestowed by the Lord."

She claimed to be able to see into the future, hear people's thoughts, visit souls who had passed away, detect ailments in animals, levitate and travel in her astral body, and rapidly assimilate huge amounts of information, such as new languages and texts. She also claimed to have insight into her previous lives: "One of the highest experiences of my existence occurred about 500,050 years ago, during the Dvapara Yuga, the period of time which was before the Kali Yuga. I received transcendental Vedic knowledge direct from the mouth of Bhagavan Lord Krishna" (44).

In addition to documenting the arduous aspects of spiritual transformation and the powers Alice experienced, much of *Monument Eternal* was an attempt to share the joy of a personal devotional relationship with God. Here, and elsewhere in her writings, she stressed the necessity of establishing and maintaining this relationship. Along with belief in the soul's divinity, this formed the core of her theology. Quite often, she lapsed into ecstatic language reminiscent of Sufi poetry to describe the intimacy she felt with the divine:

> The Lord often tells the spiritually awakened ones about divine light and universal love, by stating to them that "Mother earth loves to feel your bare feet upon her breast, the wind loves your face, your hair . . . the sun loves the measurements of your back; flowers and other plant spirits rejoice upon receiving natural rain, or water. Trees swing and sway with joy when I assume the form of the initiating spirit who will bring forth the blossoms of spring and the fruits of summer. (11)

To close the book, she wrote:

> What is monumental and eternal to me is to feel the Lord's play and hear the Lord's laughter or talk. Why, just this morning the Lord said to me: "Hey Turiya,
>
> At dawn, sit at the Feet of Action.
> At noon, be at the Hand of Might.
> At eventide, be so big, that sky will learn Sky." (53)

While the path to self-realization required establishing a personal, loving relationship with the Lord, God was for Alice a universal concept that lay outside any single religious tradition. In the faith that she followed, the Lord was manifest in a multitude of names and forms: Krishna, Rama, Jesus, and the Buddha were all valid incarnations. And, by extension, all religions were viable paths to God-realization. This notion is quite unlike that of her Christian upbringing. In the Baptist faith, God is transcendent, and the only way of finding union with him is through Jesus Christ, the redeemer. By contrast, Alice's view of God as both "one and many" is foundational to Hindu theology and finds its basis in the verse from the Rig-

Veda: "the Truth is one, the wise call it by many names."[1] For instance, concerning the oneness of God, Alice wrote:

> I am all that there is. There is naught beside Me, or like unto Me. There is naught beyond beneath or around Me, other than My Own Self. Apart from Me, no man, cosmic god, or whatsoever else knows or can measure the length, breadth or depth of my Being, and no man, cosmic god, or aught whatsoever else know or can probe the magnitude, volume or the depth of My Excellences, Glories, or My Mysteries, in as much as I am higher than the highest height, deeper than the deepest depth, vaster than the vastest expanse, and I am extended above the transcendent to the comprehension of all created minds. (1981, 37)

Concerning "the manyness of God," she wrote:

> Millions of Forms have I, and millions of formless forms have I, nonetheless My billions of Names far surpass them all for verily more than the stars in the firmament, more than the worlds in the universes, more than all the living entities therein and more than all of the atoms in the vast expanse of space therefrom are My wondrous infinite Names. (ibid. 187)

Guru and Community

In the early 1970s, Alice moved to California and began to share her convictions with other spiritual aspirants. Inspired by her writings and her example, a small group soon gathered to chant with her and study the philosophy of Vedanta in the Bay Area. From the outset, *satsang*, or community worship, consisted of singing Alice's adaptations of *bhajans*, studying Vedic texts, and listening to her spiritual discourse. This has remained the central community practice ever since.

As her following expanded, Alice founded the Vedantic Center in 1972, which was initially housed in a San Francisco storefront. In the mid-1970s, she moved to Woodland Hills, California, and reestablished the Vedantic Center next door to her home. Many of her students from the Bay Area followed, to pursue her teachings and continue their worship together. In 1983, Alice purchased fifty acres in Agoura Hills, a town neighboring Woodland Hills (where she continued to reside), and founded what was then called Shanti Anantam Ashram as a place where her students could live and worship together according to the core principles taught at the Vedantic Center.

During the late 1980s, Alice had a revelation in which Sathya Sai Baba was declared the true avatar of the age. Consequently, in 1994, Shanti Anantam Ashram was reinaugurated as the Sai Anantam Ashram, which, in effect, made it a Sathya Sai Baba affiliate. Sathya Sai Baba is an Indian guru with an international following of several million people, most of them South Asian.[2] With its focus on singing during *satsang,* or religious gatherings, which include *bhajans* sung in honor of Sai Baba, Alice's ashram is similar to other Sai Baba centers. However, in all other respects it is unique, and it functions autonomously as a nonprofit organization. The ashram's mission statement reads:

> The Ashram serves as a sanctuary where seekers of all faiths can receive and experience the sublime teachings on spiritual life. Students and residents of the Ashram are instructed to reflect spiritual values of modest dress, vegetarian diet and correct ethical behavior. The practices include meditation, scripture study, selfless service and chanting of God's Holy Names. (http://www.saiquest.com, accessed June 13, 2009)

In addition, Alice's writings, not those of Sai Baba, provide the creed at the ashram:

> The Sai Anantam Ashram appreciates the contributions of spiritual wisdom and insight from other faiths and religions. Studies undertaken at the ashram include not only Vedantic or Vedic scriptures, the oldest of the world's literatures, but also exemplary narratives and scriptural texts from more recent revelations of God found in the Bible and in the Islamic and Buddhist texts.
>
> The Vedas teach that the purpose of human birth is for making *spiritual advancement toward the highest perfectional stage of life*, which is devotional service rendered unto the Supreme Lord. Charity, kindness, selfless service, spiritual discipline and a dedicated life of devotion can bring one toward the supreme goal of life and attainment of divine realization of the Supreme Lord . . .
>
> A serious disciple who engages in dedicated, devotional service daily, who is selfless, moral, meditative, tranquil, disciplined and reverentially given unto the recitation of japam, mantram, and prayers I shall sanction it be that such a soul may go forth onward unto achievement of the Supreme Goal of divine realization. (1981, 70)[3]

Alice's paramount role as guru further distinguishes Sai Anantam Ashram from other Sathya Sai Baba centers. While Alice's students read Satya Sai Baba's discourses, revere him as an avatar, and made pilgrimages with her to India to see him, until Alice's death she was their personal guru, Alice, the one who answered their questions, looked after their spiritual well-being, and encouraged their spiritual progress on regular basis. To capture the appeal that Alice had for her students and their faith in her, I offer the words of Radha Reyes-Botafasina, a student who currently lives at the ashram and has been following her guidance for nearly thirty years:

> Swamini was a God-realized being, which is not to be taken lightly. We felt so fortunate to be in her presence . . . What she gave, what she taught us was skills: how to live in this world and the world beyond this world—how to relate to people, how to serve people. She taught us to understand that life is not a fairy tale. You have

challenges because *maya* [illusion] is there. Confronting those obstacles, that's your job. In India, you see someone down and out, and they'll say, "Well, that's my karma." Here in the West everything is supposed to follow this rosy plan. And when you're challenged you don't expect it, you don't understand the reason for the challenge.

There's nobody like Swamini. She was the blessed reassurance, and the blessed assurance as well. Because anything that ever needed to be resolved, well, the buck would stop right there. Swamini said it. It was good enough. There was no questioning. For our family lives, for our children, for their needs, whatever it was. You know, we do what we have to do as human beings, practically, but if we needed more divine guidance, this was it . . .

She always knew the answers, it was whether or not she was supposed to tell you at the time. She would encourage us to "please meditate first. Don't be so dependent!" And then, if you have a question on your meditation, on what you've seen in your meditation, then you can ask, but at least you've made the effort. She would always say on Sundays, "pray that you can go beyond salvation, beyond liberation, beyond self-realization, go all the way to God realization." You know, it's not easy. (interview with author, 2007)

Ms. Reyes-Botafasina's comments may seem out of the ordinary in our culture; however, in the Hindu tradition, gurus are accepted figures who act as conduits to divine knowledge. In their role as enlightened teachers, they facilitate the spiritual advancement of their students. In India, the guru-disciple relationship is common. In America, however, having a guru tends to be an alien concept, perhaps even a mistrusted one. This may be due to the stark individualism of Anglo-American Protestantism, but it is probably also a response to the cults and failed social experiments that arose during the 1970s, in which guru figures were negatively implicated. Although herself a celebrity, Alice seems to have escaped the scandal and notoriety that has plagued many other leaders of alternative spiritual communities. This is partly due to the fact that she kept the life of the ashram well under the public's radar screen, a feat made possible by her generous financial backing, which meant that the community did not need to attract new members or raise funds for the upkeep of the ashram's land and infrastructure.

Over the last several decades, members of the community have included both ashram residents and those who live elsewhere but come to services weekly. Most are black, middle-class, educated adults, though there are European Americans and Asian Americans. Those living at the ashram now number roughly twenty. When Alice came to play the organ and deliver her spiritual discourse for Sunday services in the summer of 2002, I counted roughly fifty people in attendance. Today, with their guru no longer living, attendance at services is dwindling.

In addition to maintaining the ashram worship and study schedule, and carrying out various community services—such as taking care of the grounds and the temple, working in the bookstore, and answering correspondence—adult members hold day jobs. They live in separate rented family units, as individuals or married couples, and their children go to local schools. Far from cultish, their lives are like those of most people in America except for their commitment to spiritual life at the ashram. I should also add that a number of community members are or were professional musicians. With their own musical backgrounds, they maintained the daily musical rituals when Swamini was not present during her lifetime, and they now continue the practice of *bhajans* in her absence.

Swamini's Bhajans

During the early stages of her life as a swami, Alice never required that her students sing in a particular manner. As with her jazz sidemen, she wished her devotees to experience freedom of expression. Nonetheless, most of her students were African American, and their devotional singing evolved in a culturally specific manner. In her adaptations of Hindu hymns, Alice made arrangements that complemented what she termed the Southern singing style of her spiritual community. She described her creative philosophy in a 1988 interview with Dolores Brandon. Referring to *Radha Krsna Nama Sankirtana* (1977), the first album on which Alice recorded her devotees, Brandon asked: "the other thing I really like about that album is that you brought a black, soul, gospel feeling too—are you aware of that?" Alice replied:

> Oh many people say that. And you know why that happens? In music, I don't think I have real preferences about form. Especially when it comes to a religious faith or a spiritual conviction. Because when you express your heart, it has to come from you. When those chants are sung I don't tell them, if you don't sound like India, forget it. I don't say such a thing. Sing the chants the way you feel about singing them. Sing from your heart and spirit and that's what you get. A number of people that were members or disciples at the Vedantic Center had that background, like a Southern kind of background and the experiences in the Baptist church. So you begin to hear that. So the music that I play basically complemented that. Because, also, my background in this lifetime, I had extensive experience playing for various churches for all kinds of faiths. The Adventists, the Baptists, the Methodists. I had a great time playing in Detroit in the various churches so I had that experience. If people had preference to hymns, and they, say, were part of our center, and they expressed like that, then the music would have that form. Again, the music would always complement the congregation that was singing, the congregational chanting. So that's why it comes out that way. And then I find out that when there are more people and they become members, and they come from various backgrounds, like especially today, eleven years later, there are people from all over—Europe, Asia.

You get such a mixture. But you're singing from your heart, your spirit. That's what I'm concerned about. (A. Coltrane 1988)

In some respects, the *bhajans* diverge substantially from Alice's professional and commercial musical projects. Her instrumentation, arrangements, and harmonic foundations are comparatively simple; they consist of keyboard, vocals, and hand percussion, with simple pentatonic melodies set over conventional chord progressions. At a deeper level, however, there are many similarities between the *bhajans* and Alice's previous works. Using methods similar to those in her jazz sessions, Alice created flexible, expandable musical structures over which individuals could elaborate or improvise their own lines. She also arranged harmonies and parts for her choir in a spontaneous fashion, particularly during studio recordings. As Reyes-Botafasina explained:

She would give us harmonies right there on the spot. She would sing it, we would be in sections, and she would come over—altos, tenors, sopranos, bari[tone]s, and one person who had a little bit of musical skills would make sure they got those notes right. The whole job of that person, poor thing, was to make sure they transmit those notes to other people and that they all sing them. And for me it was so much fun. It was like avant-garde music, completely in the moment. So, on the technical side, you are using your skills to analyze what she's giving you, you know, music is in patterns, so you can give it back. But then you listen, and . . . it's, it's so ancient, so ancient. (interview with author, 2007)

One can also equate the flexible, spontaneous aspect of these hymns to Alice's earlier recompositions of symphonic works that interrupt meter and form so that, as a player, she could find her "eternity" (Lerner 1982, 22) even within a Western art-music aesthetic. What makes the *bhajans* different from her professional work on the bandstand, however, is the devotional intent of all members involved. In this respect, Alice was returning to the congregational aesthetics of her childhood. This devotional, unmediated quality at the core of her *bhajan* practice is founded on the historical *bhajan* practice in India. In fact, it is this very ecstatic essence—related to bhakti, or personal devotion to a particular deity—that attracted Alice in the first place, and ultimately provided the grounds for her musical synthesis.

Bhajan is a generic term that refers to Hindu devotional hymns associated with bhakti revival movements throughout India's medieval period (600–1500). As a result of religious revivalism during that period, the role of the priestly class and the importance of formal religious rituals were de-emphasized and replaced by a belief that the individual should cultivate a personal relationship with the gods and goddesses. Gradually the practice of religion passed out of the control of the Brahmin caste and into the hands of leaders of sects and gurus of any caste. This religious restructuring produced generations of religious philosophers, ecstatic sects, and poet-saints who have advocated many different methods of bhakti worship.[4] Bhakti worship is typically characterized by approaching spiritual union through acts of divine love and devotion, ritual offerings, and the repetition of God's holy names.

One of most widely adopted forms of bhakti worship among Hindus is singing God's name and praising God's glories.[5] The hymns are based on ancient texts by poet-saints and usually fall in one of five categories: songs for Siva, songs for Krishna, songs for Rama, songs for the Divine Mother, and songs for the particular guru of a community. Since the sixth century, this *bhajan* tradition has been absorbed into South Asian classical arts. It has influenced Sufi and Sikh traditions of musical worship and has also remained a popular form of Hindu devotional practice. The ultimate goal of bhakti practice and the singing of *bhajans*, is to lose oneself in the love of God. This musical, emotional, and unmediated approach to worship is similar to that found in African American church services, particularly those of Baptist and Holiness congregations like the ones Alice played for as a young woman. The ecstatic nature of the genre, then, ultimately provided the basis for the unique musical synthesis one finds at Alice's ashram.

In India, particularly in the north, the practice of *bhajans* is extremely common during *satsang*, so that group singing is found at temples as well as informally in homes, where the majority of Hindu practices are daily maintained.[6] Individuals also commonly sing by themselves as they perform *puja*, the making of ritual offerings, at home altars. To facilitate group singing, *bhajan* melodies tend to be antiphonal in nature and quite simple, falling within forms of raga and tala accessible to most amateur singers.[7] Typically, an individual in the community or a professional song leader leads the worship. The usual accompaniment is harmonium and hand percussion, though one might also find other drone instruments such as a tamboura, *ektar*, or *shruti* box, and additional melodic instruments such as violin and flute.

Although the instrumentation differs, the musical forms that Alice used in her *bhajans* are quite similar to what one might encounter in India, or in other Hindu ashrams and temples in the United States. This is largely due to the structural implications suggested by the texts. *Bhajan* prosody usually conforms to or is influenced by traditional Sanskrit poetic forms. In many *bhajans*, the text consists only of the name or multiple names of a single deity. The majority of simple *bhajans* follow an AAB format, which Alice maintained, for the most part, in her adaptations. In longer *bhajans*, which have more extensive poetry, a strophic form, to which Alice also adhered, guides the musical structures. In her *japa* adaptations (the devotional genre in which singers chant the name of a single deity unaccompanied), her forms consisted only of an A section. Although these basic aspects of *bhajans* remained intact in Alice's adaptations, most of her other musical parameters reflected the aesthetics of African American music. The vocal melodies were predominantly pentatonic, set over functional chord progressions and chromatic walking bass lines. More important, the vocal idiom, group dynamics, and expressive behavior of the congregation were typical of African American ecstatic services.

Alice's *bhajan* adaptations do not mark the first use of Indian devotional songs in an American spiritual community. The earliest use of Indian devotional hymns in the United States can be traced to the English adaptations that the guru Paramahansa Yogananda introduced in the 1930s in his organization, the Self-realization Fellowship. Yogananda's hymns, however, did not follow the ecstatic tradition. They were set to Protestant melodies and sung in a staid European American fashion, similar to what one might find at a white Protestant church. A. C. Baktivedanta Prabhubada, the founder of the International Society for Krishna Consciousness in America, or ISKCON, is largely responsible for having introduced the more passionate elements of Hindu bhakti practice to the United States. The devotional chanting and singing of the ISKCON community—the repetitive *Hare Krishna, Hare Krishna, Krishna Krishna, Hare Hare* mantra—has been part of the American landscape since 1965. However, because of the eccentric and zealous manner in which ISKCON members chant in public, their particular form of musical devotion has not had wide appeal for the majority of Americans who are drawn to Hindu devotional singing.

What has become enormously popular instead, particularly over the last decade with the rise of hatha yoga, are Westernized folk-rock adaptations of Hindu devotional melodies.[8] Today, yoga studios and fitness centers play recordings of American *bhajan* singers during class and sell the music in their bookstores and boutiques. Since the 1990s, the careers of a number of American artists with Sanskrit spiritual names have blossomed: Krishna Das, Ram Das, Jai Utal, and Ma Chetan Jyoti. Today, such musicians give concerts at yoga centers, where guests are charged twenty dollars to enter. Yoga periodicals regularly advertise and review the musicians' recordings, and one can find bins of such music in CD stores. Like Alice Coltrane, many of these artists traveled to India during the late 1960s and early 1970s.

While the texts and musical forms that Alice used in her *bhajan* adaptations link her to what has become a relatively familiar devotional practice in the United States, her adaptations are quite distinct from those of American *bhajan* singers currently performing (I should mention that in America, the genre is largely known as *kirtan,* a commonly used synonym for *bhajan*).[9] For the most part, the American *bhajan* artists currently recording are itinerant singer-songwriters who play for largely white audiences. They can be seen to follow in the footsteps of American devotional singers and reform song leaders of the 1960s and 1970s who used American folk-rock idioms to spread their religious messages. By contrast, Alice's *bhajans* evolved within a specific spiritual and musical community as daily ritual music, and her arrangements served the unique expressive needs of Sai Anantam Ashram members. Her compositions were far more communally driven than those of the typical American *kirtan* song leaders, and hers were dominated by a host of African American musical elements. Additionally, Alice was not typically featured as a vocalist or lead musician on her recordings. Instead, she played a subtle, yet extremely powerful behind-the-scenes-role as an accompanist and arranger.

Although Alice began composing and recording *bhajans* as early as the mid-1970s, American followers of yoga and Hinduism have not, by and large, discovered the music. This was largely due to Alice's reluctance to perform her sacred music outside Sai Anantam Ashram. But other factors also play a part. They include the noncommercial nature of her Avatar label, which recorded most of her *bhajans* (the majority of these works are currently available only on cassette); the ecstatic African American musical elements of her devotional music, which may have scared away insular white audiences; racist attitudes about black cultural expression in general; and the fact that her early *bhajan* settings for Warner Brother were unavailable for so many years. Her adaptations, then, predated the current *bhajan* craze by at least thirty years, and even though they provide some of the most interesting stylistic fusions and deeply rapturous versions of the American *bhajan* genre available, they are little known.

Ritual

While Alice's *bhajans* appear to be a rather straightforward musical fusion of African American and South Asian devotional genres, as ritual they are much more complex. They should not be confused with forms of religious syncretism in which preexisting beliefs are grafted onto or camouflaged by hegemonic modes of religious expression, as in the case of Brazilian Candomblé or Cuban Santeria. Rather, what we encounter in Alice's *bhajans* is a fusion of culturally specific musical aesthetics with an emergent, sui generis, and subcultural belief system.

Bhajans at Sai Anantam Ashram "act out the insights and understandings," to use Albanese's words, of Alice's universalist spiritual philosophy.

On an expressive level, Christian music has come to pervade the Indian ritual. However, the Christian ideology or creed associated with gospel-music worship is no longer in play. At Sai Anantam Ashram, Jesus is not seen as the only savior but as one of many avatars, along with Rama, Krishna, Gandhi, and Sathya Sai Baba, who have descended to earth to enlighten mankind. Surya Botafasina, who is Radha Reyes-Botafasina's son and a fine young pianist raised at the ashram, explained:

> Really, I find the struggle for me is being able to explain what exactly the experience of growing up on the ashram is to other people. And so I found that through inquiries and direction, you say, "I was raised in a spiritual community." The Vedic texts and the Bhagavad-Gita are studied and heard from on a frequent basis. The devotional songs we sing, *bhajans*, are mostly in Sanskrit; however, we celebrate Christmas, we love Jesus, we love anything that has to do with God, period. And it's just a really great experience and a great privilege to be able to be a part of the most high. (interview with author, 2002)

Botafasina and other ashram members are clearly aware of the musical hybridity of these chants; they nonetheless view them as "ancient," universal, and transcendent. Botafasina explained: "You can break it down and say there are various elements—that sounds like a gospel riff, or that sounds like a jazz change, or that sounds like a really funky bass line, or that sounds like a really Indian thing. But in the end, it's just music from the real source, number one, God" (ibid.).

For ashram members, *bhajan* practice achieves a set of spiritual ends that are consistent with Alice's theology: *bhajan* practice helps the chanter establish a personal relationship with God, calms and focuses the mind as a form of mantra meditation, and offers the chanter an experience of totality or universal consciousness. Alice stated on the ashram's website: "Chanting is a universal devotional engagement, one that allows the chanter to soar to higher realms of spiritual consciousness. Chanting is a healing force for good in our world, and also in the astral worlds. Chanting can bring a person closer to God because that person is calling on the Lord" (http://www.saiquest.com, accessed August 2003). She also wrote: "*Bhajan* chanting extols the magnificence and the holiness of God. It celebrates the divine glories of the Lord. Chanting consists of worshipping God through song and music . . . Chanting removes agitations or *vrittis* from the mind, and brings peace. It edifies one, uplifts the spirit, purifies the atmosphere, and elevates the consciousness" (1999, 4).

Botafasina wrote about the experience of chanting:

> It is a very interesting phenomenon to hear each singer and the personal special connection that he or she has with God through the music. Many a day have I been

driven to tears when participating in the *bhajans*. The passion that one's soul has for its source overrides all other thoughts or feelings which could even be close to being deemed as secular or materialistic. During these refrains, the Names are being exalted in most heavenly ways. The timeless spirit of the ancient beings can be felt. Many significant, memorable spiritual experiences are often recalled at these times . . . Whether you are at the workplace toiling in a job which tests your patience, at home performing your own personal *puja*, singing during selfless service to mankind, or keeping the Names of the Lord on your mind as you proceed throughout your day, *bhajans* enhance the atmosphere. *Bhajans* can be felt long after the chord has been played. The mind may forget, but the heart always wants to hear more of its heavenly home. (Botafasina 2001)

His mother described her experience of chanting in this fashion:

What's important—what's unique—is what's going on with the consciousness of the person chanting *bhajans* in the *mandir* [temple]. What kind of visions you are having? Everything was being answered that you wanted to have answered. It's all there in this chanting. The ecstasy, the understanding, all at once. It's an incredible experience. You get chills all over. We would sing until we couldn't sing anymore. We would chant so much that we couldn't talk anymore. We could only say, "Om Namah, Sivaya." And that was the whole purpose—for the *bhajans* to ultimately become mantra. It's beyond all the musical elements. (Reyes-Botafasina interview with author, 2007)

Through daily communal repetition, *bhajans* have become a tradition in their own right. Ashram members do not experience *bhajans* as if they were performing the compositions of Alice Coltrane. For instance, Botafasina was absorbing a specific musical vocabulary and an approach to making music that many would associate with the gospel and jazz traditions. However, he does not have this personal connection to these traditions. For him, these practices are associated with the *bhajans* he has grown up with and the spiritual practices of the ashram. Through repetition and their relationship to a sacred space and a devotional community, *bhajans* have become tradition for him and are felt to be timeless and eternal. Consider his following comment: "I love Herbie Hancock, especially the tune 'Maiden Voyage,' but I didn't know the true meaning of a sus chord [suspended chord] until I heard it in a *bhajan*. Okay, in *bhajans* you know you will stay in that one key [laughs], just rest there, and well, twenty minutes will have gone by—we're still singing" (interview with author, 2002).

For Botafasina, the act of singing *bhajans* also serves to "bring the community together." In this communal context, each member testifies to his or her experience through song. The act of singing, then, functions in both an individual and collective sense to validate and encourage the faith of the congregation. Botafasina likened the experience to a family reunion:

The ashram always feels like a family gathering on Sunday afternoons. Various sopranos and rich altos can be heard singing *Jai!!!! Hari!!!! Krishna!!!! Rama!!!!! Sathya Sai!!!!! Sathya Sai Ghana Shyama!!!!* All of the names reach the trees, mountains, land, stream, and animals in the near proximity. The males with their booming baritones, and textured tenor voices all bellowing *Bham Bham Bolo!!!!! Jai Shri Ram!!!! Siva Shankara!!!!!!* Oh pity me, words never could accurately describe the joy I am trying to convey on this paper. Even if I were able to play a CD on a state-of-the-art sound system, the feeling could only be replicated not duplicated. It is truly an experience, which is unique to the *bhajans* of that land. Swaminiji has stated "the *bhajans* in this mandir are sung like no other place in the Universe." (Botafasina 2001)

Sacred Circle

It is now almost two years since Alice's "ascension" and her students continue their involvement in this ritualized *bhajan* practice. Their sustained involvement points not only to her success in structuring communal spiritual life at the ashram, but also to her powerful and influential role as guru in their lives. What I have found extraordinary in speaking with Surya Botafasina and his mother about *bhajans* at the ashram is the way that Alice succeeded in providing them with an experience of music making that drew directly from the experiences of her own life. She reproduced the interrelationship of music, family, community, love of God, and the aesthetics of ecstatic black music characteristic of her formative years in Detroit. She also maintained an approach to musical worship that reflects John Coltrane's theory of music's universal, transcendent nature, and she incorporated elements of Hindu practice learned in the company of her gurus and during her travels to India.

Ultimately, Alice succeeded in creating a unique devotional practice based on the wide-ranging and rich experiences of her life. And her *bhajans* act as ritual still. Functioning as such, they "act out the insights and understandings" that are expressed in the ashram's spiritual philosophy, they "serve to bring the community together," and they structure the daily lives of members (Albanese 1999, 10). *Bhajans* are intertwined with the belief that as a form of bhakti practice, they lead to God-realization. They are also central to the sense of community, with singing bringing the ashram together twice a day and collectively confirming each individual's spiritual path.

With these *bhajans*, Alice Coltrane completed a sacred circle and returned to the congregational aesthetics of her youth. In many respects, however, she never really left them. Even when recording projects that were ostensibly secular or commercial in nature, she found a way to make them personal vehicles for worship and transcendence. Additionally, the musical environments she participated in always communally validated individual experience. This was true of her bebop engagements, her avant-garde jazz projects with her husband, and her own compositions. Her music was always, to use her words, "spiritual music." Central to the gospel services of her childhood, her impulse to testify developed into a highly refined and eclectic philosophy of musical transcendence in the company of figures such as John Coltrane and her Indian spiritual teachers.

As a professional musician, Alice inspired those with whom she played with her sensitivity, virtuosity, and wide-ranging abilities as a multi-instrumentalist. As a composer, she never tired of exploring new sounds, traditions, and technologies. As the musical and spiritual anchor of Sai Anantam Ashram, she brought happiness, well-being, and strength to her disciples and to everyone she met. As a woman, she led an adventurous and fortunate life in which family, community, professional success, and spiritual practice were integrated.

How many people realize their potential to this extent? How many are able to watch their creative imagination unfold so vividly? How many musicians hear their compositions in the hands of master players, and in the hearts and voices of their students as devotional ritual? How many people invent traditions that outlive them? Alice is a rare example. Her boundary-crossing aesthetics and her inspiring spiritual autobiography—documented in sound, text, and ritual—tells a free story, testifying to her faith and extraordinary personal history. Perhaps most of all, it reveals an understanding of herself that transcends earthly constructions.

Notes

Introduction

1 For instance, in Ken Burns's popular documentary *Jazz: A History of America's Music* (2000), as well as in the film *The Story of Jazz* (1993), the contributions of John Coltrane represent the end of jazz's stylistic evolution. The divergent genres since the late 1960s, such as fusion and free jazz, are commonly viewed as ruptures in tradition. Post-Coltrane musicians are commonly presented outside the fold. See, for instance, Gridley 1991.

2. See James 1999, which calls attention to the radicalism of "black protofeminists" such as Sojourner Truth and Harriet Tubman.

3. Bernice Johnson Reagon, a founding member of the musical group Sweet Honey and the Rock, has published several musicological works that explore African American vocal traditions. See Reagon 1992, 2001.

4. See James 1999, hooks 1981, and Wallace 1982.

5. Sun Ra was perhaps the only other jazz musician who had this kind of iconoclastic and otherworldly persona. For a comprehensive study of Sun Ra's music and his mysticism, see Szwed 1997.

6. See, for example, Koskoff 2001.

7. Drawing on the concept of hegemony, Slobin calls attention to the ways in which these structures are both internalized and contested.

8. For a further account of the place of testifying in African American culture, see Smitherman 1986.

9. Historical overviews that have been crucial to my research include Jean Humez's edition of Jackson 1981, Andrews 1986, and Collier-Thomas 1998.

10. Haywood appropriates the term "prophesying" to describe this justice-oriented aspect of their work and defines prophesying as "a perceived mandate from God to spread his word in order to advance a conscious or unconscious political agenda" (17).

11. See Foster 1993, Braxton 1989, and Douglass Chin 2001.

12. "Womanist" is a word Alice Walker (1982) coined to refer to a bold, spiritually minded, and humanistic brand of feminism resulting from the African American experience.

13. See the works cited in the previous footnote, as well as Connor 1991 and Baker, Alexander, and Redmond 1991.

14. Music historians have discussed this persistent attitude toward black Christian worship. For instance, writing on the early cultural contact between whites and blacks, Eileen Southern has stated: "nowhere in the history of black experience in the United States was the clash of cultures-the African versus the European-more obvious than in the differing attitudes taken toward ritual dancing and spirit possession" (Southern 1983, 171). For a discussion of the strategies jazz writers have used to make jazz a highbrow art, see DeVeaux 1991.

15. See, for example, Jost 1974, Dean 1992, and Litweiler 1993.

16. See, for instance, Baraka 1963 and 1970, Sidran 1971, and Kofsky 1998.

17. Scholars who have made preliminary inquiries into the political dimensions of the spiritual jazz of the sixties include Kelley 2002 and Monson 2007.

1. God's Child in the Motor City

The epigraph to this chapter quotes from my 2001 interview with Alice Coltrane.

1. See Sugrue 1996, 43, for a discussion of Detroit's reputation as "the northernmost Southern City."

2. These and later population figures are from the U.S. Bureau of the Census.

3. Prior to the Great Migration of blacks from the South, between 1915 and 1930, most of the roughly 6,000 blacks in Detroit belonged to what W.E.B. Du Bois called the "talented tenth." This small upper class were educated professionals-lawyers, doctors, schoolteachers and members of the clergy-who earned a good income and lived in "well-appointed homes" (Ricks 1960, 98). By 1920, the community had changed dramatically. According to the U.S. Bureau of the Census, more than 40,000 blacks lived in Detroit at that time, and most were struggling families.

4. See "Detroit is Dynamite" 1942 and Shogan and Craig 1964.

5. During the first two decades of the twentieth century, African American families shared their blocks with other European immigrant groups-predominantly Jews from various countries and Christian Poles. However, by the thirties, the white community had become competitive and hostile, perceiving the swelling numbers of poor Southern blacks as an economic and racial threat. Housing discrimination, intimidation, and episodic violence pushed the black population into densely settled areas. For a detailed explanation of this transformation over several decades, as well as specific incidents such the Ossian Sweet story, see Sugrue 1996.

6. In an interview with me, Vishnu Wood described this type of neighborhood affiliation. Bjorn and Gallert 2001 also mentions the East-West divide and its meaning for musicians.

7. For instance, Mukenge writes that "racial and class interests coincide to the extent that the black population remains largely undifferentiated . . . differentiation of the black population is an urban phenomenon brought on by economic, political and consequent demographic factors which reached their peak in the first quarter of the twentieth century" (1983, 26).

8. See Sugrue's discussion on housing shortages (1996, 41).

9. Here I use the word "spiritual" to refer to religious folk songs composed by African Americans before or outside their involvement with white Christian religious institutions. These songs, according to Ricks, are of three types: spirituals, which are sad in mood; jubilees, which are happy in mood; and shouts, which are used for dancing and may take the form of either a spiritual or jubilee. Three other subcategories of folk songs are "moanin' songs, songs for the dead, and narrative songs" (1960, 52).

10. More specifically, these were Protestant hymns and anthems written by such composers as Isaac Watts, John Newton, and Charles Wesley during the eighteenth and early nineteenth centuries. These were rather formal compositions-lyric poems set to smooth melodies with European harmonies. Many of these works were collected and published by Richard Allen of the American Methodist Episcopal Church in 1818 and have been particularly favored by black Methodist congregations. However, these older hymns are sung in mainstream Baptist churches as well. For a detailed discussion of black Methodist hymnals, see Southern 1983, 80, and 1986. For an overview of black hymnody, see Spencer 1992.

11. These songs have been traced to the camp meetings of the Second Great Awakening. In part the product of African American musical practices that spread in the religious fervor of the meetings, the American hymnody that evolved at that time differed in its formal style from the European American kind. This genre is characterized by folk tunes adapted to an array of religious texts, "a stringing together of isolated lines from prayers, the Scriptures, and orthodox hymns, the whole made longer by the addition of choruses and the injecting of refrains between verses" (Southern 1983, 85). This repertoire most often relied upon, and featured, a song leader who was expected to improvise and embellish phrases. Call-and-response forms and wandering verses-catchy refrains that were inserted in or tagged onto more than one song-became popular among the congregants.

During the Gospel Revival Movement of the 1850s, new songs were written by black and white composers that were much like the earlier camp songs in their formal style and their incorporation of popular melodies. Two evangelical crusaders, Dwight Lyman Moody and Ira David Sankey, collected many of the older camp songs and the new gospel compositions and published them in 1875 in *Gospel Hymns and Sacred Songs*, which became popular in the cities among both blacks and whites. While American hymnody by Moody and Sankey fell out of favor in many white Protestant churches, black Baptist, black Methodist, and independent black denominations maintained the use of this mid-nineteenth-century gospel repertoire.

12. For an examination of the style of early gospel music, see Boyer 1984.

13. Southern writes: "The year 1921 brought a milestone in the history of black-church hymnody. In my opinion, *Gospel Pearls*, published that year by the Sunday School Publishing Board of the National Baptist Convention, U.S.A., ranks with Richard Allen's hymnal of 1801 in terms of its historic importance. Like the Allen hymnal, it is an anthology of the most popular black-church music of its time. The Music Committee that compiled the hymnal . . . included some of the nation's out-

standing composers and performers of religious music . . . and the result was truly a soul-stirring message-bearing song-book" (1986, 156).

14. For a detailed description of the contents of *Gospel Pearls,* see Southern 1983, 450–51).

15. Southern 1983 uses the term "folk church," and Ricks (1960) uses the term "shouting churches" to designate African American Christian churches independent of the mainstream black Baptist and Methodist denominations.

16. Ricks 1960 is the only scholar I have found who attempts to provide a genealogy of folk music types that form the basis of urban gospel music (1960).

17. A mention of the 1970s Art Davis and Earl Madison affair with the New York Philharmonic is in order here, since this was one of the major public cases of racism in orchestral employment, and it led to the adoption of new standards and practices for auditions. It was Madison and Davis who suggested that they and other applicants play behind screens to remove any possibility of racism in the selection process. This is now a standard practice.

18. For a detailed cultural and historical analysis of ballroom dancing as popular entertainment in America, see Erinberg 1981.

19. Detroit's famous McKinney's Cotton Pickers was one of the first black dance bands to play for white audiences. For a detailed examination of racial politics and jazz culture in Detroit during the teens and twenties, see Bjorn and Gallert 2001.

20. For a lengthy discussion of Paradise Valley's musical heyday and its subsequent demise due to urban renewal, see Bjorn and Gallert 2001.

21. It should be noted that both Milt Jackson and Lucky Thompson, two former Detroiters, played in the pioneering bands of Parker and Gillespie during the period.

22. There has been little scholarly discussion of regional variation in bebop styles. The pervasive and monolithic bebop narrative implies that its New York-based progenitors sought critical distance from the notion of jazz as dance or entertainment music. In Detroit, however, the bebop approach was seldom divorced from the blues-based, dance-music continuum. For a discussion of the origins and development of bebop, its growing distinction as art music, and its use as cultural capital within New York's beatnik subculture, see DeVeaux 1997.

23. As relayed to Mark Slobin in conversation with Kenny Burrell.

24. Personal accounts such as Davis's *Miles: The Autobiography* (1989), as well as journalism and jazz criticism-which call attention to the more degrading aspects of the entertainment business and jazz culture-are responsible for such stereotypical associations. For an examination of the trope of the jazz musician as socially deviant, see Monson 1995.

25. Miles Davis came to Detroit to kick his habit, knowing that heroin in Detroit was harder to find than in New York. For a detailed account of his time in Detroit, see Bjorn and Gallert 2001, 133–38.

26. Family musical lineages have been particularly important to the early careers of female jazz musicians, offering them professional exposure that might not otherwise have been available due to sexism in the professional world, religious and bour-

geois values that curtail women's mobility beyond the sphere of domesticity, and the potential dangers encountered as an itinerant entertainer.

27. For a discussion of housing patterns in Detroit, see Sugrue 1996.

28. This quote is taken from an unpublished interview with Lars Bjorn and used with his permission.

29. Alice's brother, Jackie McLeod, told me this in a conversation at Baker's Keyboard Lounge, in Detroit, in November 2000.

30. For a detailed ethnography of Detroit's West Side clubs, see Bjorn and Gallert 2001.

31. Full transcriptions of Alice Coltrane's solos with Terry Gibbs are available on the Wesleyan University Press website.

2. Manifestation

The epigraph to this chapter is quoted from my 2001 interview with Alice Coltrane.

1. John Junior died tragically young in an automobile accident in 1985.

2. In 1970, several years after John Coltrane passed away, Alice played harp on Tyner's album *Extensions.*

3. Despite the diverse styles of post-1950s jazz, avant-garde musicians have been generally distinguished from the mainstream jazz community by their explorations of free meter, free-form, and group improvisation. However, within the first and second generation of avant-garde players, such as Ornette Coleman, Cecil Taylor, and Charles Mingus, and in the music of their disciples, variable "formative principles" have distinguished their styles (Jost 1974, 9). The aesthetics of "free" music have therefore been extremely difficult to categorize as a whole. David Such explains "free" jazz as a general need to lessen restrictions on various formal elements of jazz. He equates the jazz avant-garde with contemporary movements in modernist painting that have explored texture, structure, and new mediums (1993, 28). The free-jazz community has also been associated with a postmodern creative philosophy, summarized in statements such as this: "free jazz is a music without boundaries; or is genre-less, so to speak. Any process of creating, transmitting or learning music, and the assimilation of any external influence, from any geographical location, past, present, or future, is possible" (Kiroff 1997,18).

4. "Cool" jazz is a highly amorphous musical category. As a racialized term, it typically refers to the soft aesthetics of white, "West Coast" players such as the trumpeter Chet Baker and the saxophonists Stan Getz and Paul Desmond. However, the concept of "cool" is also associated with Miles Davis and his late modal approach, typified on the 1958 album *Kind of Blue* as well as in Davis's orchestral projects in collaboration with the composer-arrangers Claude Thornhill and Gill Evans. Here, I am referring to works that purposely make use of the gospel idiom, a subgenre of hard-bop often called "soul jazz."

5. See, for instance, Murray 1976, Boyer 1977, Levine 1977, Maultsby 1992, Hersch 1995–96, and Ramsey 2003.

6. See Weinstein 1992 and Turner 1997.

7. Don Ellis, Paul Horn, and John McLoughlin are some of the more influential white jazz musicians to have explored South Asian religions. For a comprehensive overview, see Farrell 1997.

8. Sun Ra was perhaps the only other jazz musician to attempt this kind of project at the time. However, Ra's personal eccentricities in dress and demeanor, his unconventional "intergalactic" orchestra, and his lack of backing in the recording industry resulted in his comparative obscurity. Coltrane visited Sun Ra several times in Chicago in the late 1950s. Ra claims that he was the first to inspire Coltrane to follow this path of musical and spiritual transcendence. See, for instance, Ra's comments in the documentary *Tell Me How Long Trane's Been Gone* (2001). For a comprehensive study of Sun Ra's music and his own brand of mysticism, see Szwed 1997.

9. See Tynan 1965.

10. See Olatunji's remarks in *Tell Me How Long Trane's Been Gone* (2001).

11. One can reasonably argue that John Coltrane developed this creative approach with previous musical mentors such as Miles Davis, or that he took cues from avant-garde pioneers like Ornette Coleman and Albert Ayler. Regardless, when this philosophy of self-expression is manifested in Alice's avant-garde music, it immediately triggers an association with her husband's artistic example and their relationship.

12. H. Richard Niebuhr first articulated this manner of social organization in his classic study *The Social Sources of Denominationalism* (1929).

13. See, for example, Levine 1977, Maultsby 1985, Wilson 1992, and Floyd 1995,

14. Though dealing almost exclusively with European American culture, several authors have taken up the issue of American interest in Eastern spirituality during the 1960s. See Cox 1977; Wuthnow 1978 and 1998; Ellwood 1979, 1987, and 1994; Tipton 1981; and Prashad 2000.

15. While McAlister's focus is on the Nation of Islam, her insights and observations can be extended to other forms of non-Western spirituality.

3. Universal Consciousness

1. Many of the sections of *Monument Eternal* read much like Paramahansa Yoganadanda's *Autobiography of a Yogi* (1946), a mystical text from India's yogic tradition in which the aspirant-writer endures a series of mental and physical tests. John Coltrane had a copy of the book in his library-it was a very popular book at the time-and it is likely that he passed it on to Alice.

2. One visit in particular has acquired the stature of legend among practitioners of Integral Yoga. Apparently unbeknownst to Alice, the Integral Yoga Institute needed an additional $3,000 to buy what is now its building on West Thirteenth Street. Alice was visiting Swami Satchidananda the afternoon that the sale was being negotiated, and she accidentally left her checkbook behind. When she returned to fetch it, an hour before the deal was to fall through, she spontaneously left a donation for exactly $3,000. Today members of the institute believe this gift to have been the result of divine intervention.

3. See Thurman 1979.

4. For a comprehensive overview, see Farrell 1997. Other jazz artists who have explored various sects of Japanese Buddhism and have acknowledged the aesthetic influence of their spiritual practice in interviews and liner notes include Herbie Hancock and Wayne Shorter. Yusef Lateef's involvement with Ahmadiyya Islam and Dizzy Gillespie's practice of Bahai have surfaced in interviews and in biographical sketches.

5. The Hindu philosopher and writer Sri Shankara (788–820) is responsible for establishing Advaita Vedanta as the dominant Hindu philosophical tradition.

6. This quote is taken from the liner notes to *Universal Consciousness* (1971).

7. Dvorak is renowned for having argued during this period that America should develop its own national school of music based on the folk music of its native peoples and traditions. He was also extremely interested in promoting and educating black American composers. See Beckerman 2003.

4. Glorious Chants

1. I have borrowed this notion of "one and many" from the Hindu religion scholar Diana Eck. For a thoughtful comparative study of Christianity and Hinduism and a discussion of this theological position, see Eck 1993, 53.

2. He has become a highly influential public figure in India, partly because of his supposed miracles and partly because of his reported good works-he has founded numerous charities, medical clinics, and educational centers throughout India. His organization claims to have over 30,000 centers around the world working to extend his message and ministry. The main center is Sai Baba's village ashram in Puttaparthi, India, which houses an airport to facilitate the tens of thousands of devotees who come annually to pay their respects. His miracles include materializing sugar candy, flowers, *vibhuti* (sacred ashes), and other presents for his devotees; they also include healing the sick and knowing the thoughts of his disciples, wherever they may be. Despite his own claims that he is divine and possesses infinite power, Sai Baba maintains that he did not come to earth to establish a religion. Rather, he sees his mission as restoring the dharma.

3. The last paragraph of this quote appears on the Sai Anantam Ashram website, quoted from A. Coltrane 1981.

4. The *Srimad-Bhagavata* and the *Vishnu Purana* describe nine forms of bhakti worship. They are *sravana* (hearing stories about God); *kirtana* (singing of God's glories); *smarana* (remembering God's name and presence); *padasevana* (service to God's feet); *archana* (worship of God); *vandana* (prostration to the Lord); *dasya* (cultivating the attitude of a servant to God); *sakhya* (cultivating friendship with God); and *atmanivedana* (complete surrender of the self).

5. Esoteric writings on mantras and music also correlate the actual sounds of Sanskrit vowels and musical pitches to specific chakras, or psychospiritual nerve centers. Some *bhajan* practitioners believe that regular devotional singing can stimulate and awaken *shakti,* or divine energy, in the physical body. See Padoux 1990.

6. Because of its lengthy history, ubiquity, and regional diversity, it is possible to offer only the barest outline of traditional *bhajan* practice here.

7. Classical singers have also set the poetry of *bhajans* in more formal compositions.

8. Hatha yoga is a South Asian spiritual discipline that focuses on physical and mental control. In the United States, it has become a popular form of exercise.

9. Both in the United States and in India, the two words tend to be used interchangeably for antiphonal devotional singing, though some practitioners argue that there are subtle differences between the two genres. In Sanskrit, *kirtana* literally means telling, repeating, or praising. However, in South India, *kirtan(am)* overlaps with the *kritti* genre of art music, whose poetry is devotional in content but which is performed by soloists in classical style. To make matters slightly more confusing, both *bhajans* and *kirtan* are often confused with *nam sam kirtan*, which is the simple repetition or chanting of God's name. Though members at Sai Anantam Ashram call their hymns *bhajans,* given their variety, they are best seen as drawing from this larger pool of antiphonal devotional genres.

Bibliography

Albanese, Catherine L. *America: Religions and Religion*. Belmont, Calif.: Wadsworth, 1999.

Andrews, William L., ed. *Sisters of the Spirit: Three Black Women's Autobiographies of the Nineteenth Century*. Bloomington: Indiana University Press, 1986.

———. *To Tell a Free Story: The First Century of Afro-American Autobiography, 1760–1865*. Urbana: University of Illinois Press, 1986.

Baker, Houston A., Elizabeth Alexander, and Patricia Redmond. *Workings of the Spirit: The Poetics of Afro-American Women's Writing*. Chicago: University of Chicago Press, 1991.

Baraka, Imamu Amiri [LeRoi Jones]. *Black Music*. New York: Morrow, 1970.

———. *Blues People: Negro Music in White America*. New York: Morrow, 1963.

Beckerman, Michael B. *New Worlds of Dvorak: Searching in America for the Composer's Inner Life*. New York: Norton, 2003.

Bjorn, Lars, and Jim Gallert. *Before Motown: A History of Jazz in Detroit 1920-1960*. Ann Arbor: University of Michigan Press, 2001.

Botafasina, Surya. Interview with author. New York, November 2002. Tape and transcript in author's possession.

———. Unpublished paper. December 2001.

Bourne, Michael. "Barry Harris: Keeper of the Bebop Flame." *Down Beat* 58, no. 9 (1985): 26–28.

Boyer, Horace Clarence. "Gospel Music: Sacred or Secular?" *First World* 1 (1977): 46–49.

———. *How Sweet the Sound: The Golden Age of Gospel*. Washington, D.C.: Elliot and Clark, 1995.

———. "The 'Old Meter Hymn' and Other Types of Gospel Songs." *Views on Black American Music* 2 (1984): 41–46.

Braxton, Joanne. *Black Women Writing Autobiography: A Tradition within a Tradition*. Philadelphia: Temple University Press, 1989.

Brereton, Virginia L. *From Sin to Salvation: Stories of Women's Conversions, 1800 to the Present*. Bloomington: Indiana University Press, 1991.

Burnim, Mellonee. “Functional Dimensions of Gospel Music.” *The Western Journal of Black Studies* 12, no. 2 (1988): 112–21.

Carby, Hazel. “In Body and Spirit: Representing Black Women Musicians.” *Black Music Research Journal* 11, no. 2 (1992): 177–92.

Carner, Gary. “Pepper Adams’s Rue Serpente.” *Jazz Research* 22 (1990): 119–38.

Chambers, Paul. “Paul Chambers Talks to Valerie Wilmer.” By Valerie Wilmer. *Jazz Journal* 19, no. 3 (1961): 15–16.

Clark, Kenneth. *Dark Ghetto*. New York: Morrow, 1964.

Cleage, Albert. *Black Christian Nationalism: New Directions for the Black Church*. New York: Morrow, 1972.

Cole, Ed. “Ptah the El Daoud.” *Down Beat* 38, no. 1 (1971): 20.

Collier-Thomas, Bettye. *Daughters of Thunder: Black Women Preachers and Their Sermons*. San Francisco: Jossey-Bass, 1998.

Coltrane, Alice. “Alice Coltrane.” By Angela Dews. *Essence*, December 1971, 42–43.

———. *Divine Revelations*. Agoura Hills, Calif.: Avatar Book Institute, 1995.

———. *Endless Wisdom I*. Los Angeles: Avatar Book Institute, 1981.

———. *Endless Wisdom II*. Agoura Hills, Calif.: Avatar Book Institute 1999.

———. “The Evolution of Alice Coltrane.” Interview with Dolores Brandon. WBAI, 1988.

———. “Interview with Alice Coltrane.” By Clea McDougall. *ascent* 29 (Spring 2006): 37–41.

———. Interview with author. Woodland Hills, Calif., June 2001. Tape and transcript in author’s possession.

———. Interview with John Palmer, 1991, Avalon Archives, New York.

———. *Mantra*. Agoura Hills, Calif.: Avatar Book Institute, 1999.

———. *Monument Eternal*. Los Angeles: Vedantic Book Press, 1977.

Coltrane, John. “Entretien avec John Coltrane.” By Jean Clouzet and Michael Delorme. *Les Cahiers du Jazz*, no. 8 (1963): 1–14.

Cone, James H. *My Soul Looks Back*. Nashville: Abingdon, 1982.

Connor, Kimberly Rae. “Conversions and Visions in the Writings of African American Women.” Ph.D. diss., University of Virginia, 1991.

Cox, Harvey. *Turning East: The Promise and Peril of the New Orientalism*. New York: Simon and Schuster, 1977.

Davis, Miles, and Quincy Trope. *Miles: The Autobiography*. New York: Simon and Schuster, 1989.

Dean, Roger. *New Structures in Jazz and Improvised Music since 1960*. Philadelphia: Open University Press, 1992.

“Detroit Is Dynamite.” *Life*, August 17, 1942, 15–23.

DeVeaux, Scott. *The Birth of Bebop: A Social and Musical History.* Berkeley: University of California Press, 1997.

———. “Constructing the Jazz Tradition.” *Black American Research Literature Forum* 25, no. 3 (1991): 544–60.

Douglass Chin, Richard. *Preacher Woman Sings the Blues: The Autobiographies of*

Nineteenth-Century African American Evangelists. Columbia: University of Missouri Press, 2001.

Eck, Diana. *Encountering God: A Spiritual Journey from Bozeman to Banaras*. Boston: Beacon, 1993.

Ellwood, Robert. *Alternative Altars: Unconventional and Eastern Spirituality in America*. Chicago: University of Chicago Press, 1979.

——, ed. *Eastern Spirituality in America*. New York: Paulist Press, 1987.

——. *Mysticism and Religion*. New York: Seven Bridges, 1999.

——. *The Sixties Spiritual Awakening: American Religion Moving from Modern to Postmodern*. New Brunswick, N.J.: Rutgers University Press, 1994.

Erinberg, Lewis. *Steppin' Out: New York Nightlife and the Transformation of American Culture, 1890–1930*. Westport, Conn.: Greenwood, 1981.

Farrell, Gerry. *Indian Music and the West*. Oxford: Clarendon Press of Oxford University Press, 1997.

Fichter, Joseph H. "American Religion and the Negro." *Daedalus* 94, no. 4 (Fall 1965): 1087–1106.

Floyd, Samuel A. *The Power of Black Music: Interpreting Its History from Africa to the United States*. New York: Oxford University Press, 1995.

Foote, Julia A. *A Brand Plucked from the Fire: An Autobiographical Sketch*. Cleveland: Lauer and Yost, 1886.

Foster, Frances Smith. *Written by Herself: Literary Production by African American Women, 1746–1892*. Bloomington: Indiana University Press, 1993.

Frazier, Edward Franklin. *The Negro Church in America*. New York: Schocken, 1964.

Gibbs, Terry. Telephone interview with author. April 2001. Tape and transcript in author's possession.

——, and Cary Ginell. *Good Vibes: A Life in Jazz*. Lanham, Md.: Scarecrow, 2003.

Gridley, Mark C. *Jazz Styles: History and Analysis*. Englewood Cliffs, N.J.: Prentice Hall, 1991.

Harding, Vincent. "The Religion of Black Power." In *The Religious Situation: 1968*, edited by Donald R. Cutler, 3–31. Boston: Beacon, 1968.

Harris, Barry. "Silence and Music: An Interview with Barry Harris." By Daniel Fedele. *Jazz Changes* 2, no. 2 (Summer 1995): 16–19.

Haywood, Chanta M. *Prophesying Daughters: Black Women Preachers and the Word, 1823–1913*. Columbia: University of Missouri Press, 2003.

Henderson, Mae Gwendolyn. "Speaking in Tongues: Dialogics, Dialectics and the Black Woman Writer's Literary Tradition." In *Colonial Discourse and Post-Colonial Theory*, edited by Patrick Williams and Laura Chrisman, 257–69. New York: Columbia University Press, 1994.

Hentoff, Nat. Liner notes to *Live at the Village Vanguard!* by John Coltrane. Impulse! 1961.

Hersch, Charles. "'Let Freedom Ring'": Free Jazz and African-American Politics." *Cultural Critique*, no. 32 (Winter 1995–96): 97–123.

Hobsbawm, Eric. Introduction. In *The Invention of Tradition*, edited by Eric Hobsbawm and Terence Ranger, 1–14. Cambridge: Cambridge University Press, 1983.

hooks, bell. *Ain't I a Woman: Black Women and Feminism*. Boston: South End Press, 1981.

Humez, Jean. "An Editor's Thoughts." In *Gifts of Power: The Writings of Rebecca Jackson, Black Visionary, Shaker Eldress*, by Rebecca Jackson, 2–14. Edited by Jean Humez. Amherst: University of Massachusetts Press, 1981.

Jackson, Rebecca. *Gifts of Power: The Writings of Rebecca Jackson, Black Visionary, Shaker Eldress.* Edited by Jean Humez. Amherst: University of Massachusetts Press, 1981.

James, Joy. *Shadowboxing: Representations of Black Feminist Politics*. New York: St. Martin's, 1999.

Jenkins, Philip. *Mystics and Messiahs: Cults and New Religions in American History*. New York: Oxford University Press, 2000.

Jost, Ekkehard. *Free-Jazz*. New York: Da Capo, 1974.

Kelley, Robin D. G. *Freedom Dreams: The Black Radical Imagination*. Boston: Beacon, 2002.

Kiroff, Matthew J. "Caseworks: As Performed by Cecil Taylor and the Art Ensemble of Chicago-A Musical and Sociopolitical History." Ph.D. diss., Cornell University, 1997.

Kofsky, Frank. *John Coltrane and the Jazz Revolution of the 1960s*. 1970. Reprint, New York: Pathfinder, 1998.

Koskoff, Ellen. *Music in Lubavitcher Life*. Urbana: University of Illinois Press, 2001.

Lee, Jarena. *Religious Experience and Journal of Mrs. Jarena Lee, Giving an Account of Her Call to Preach the Gospel*. Philadelphia. 1849.

Lerner, David. "Alice Coltrane: Jazz Pianist, Inspirational Organist." *Keyboard* 8, no. 11 (November 1982): 22–27.

Levine, Lawrence W. *Black Culture and Black Consciousness: Afro-American Folk Thought from Slavery to Freedom*. New York: Oxford University Press, 1977.

Lewis, George. "Experimental Music in Black and White: The AACM in New York, 1970–1985." *Current Musicology*, no. 71–73 (Spring 2001-Spring 2002): 101–57.

Litweiler, John. "Alice Coltrane: A Monastic Trio." *Down Beat* 36, no. 3 (1969): 22.

———. *The Freedom Principle: Jazz after 1958*. New York: Quill, 1993.

———. *Ornette Coleman: A Life in Harmolodics*. New York: Da Capo, 1994.

Maultsby, Portia K. "The Impact of Gospel Music on the Secular Music Industry." In *Signifyn(g), Sanctifyn' and Slam Dunking*, edited by Gena Dagel Caponi, 172–90. Amherst: University of Massachusetts Press, 1992.

———. "West African Influences and Retentions in U.S. Black Music: A Sociocultural Study." In *More Than Dancing: Essays of Afro-American Music and Musicians*, edited by Irene V. Jackson, 9–25. Westport, Conn.: Greenwood, 1985.

Maupin, Bennie. Telephone interview with author. October 2001. Tape and transcript in author's possession.

McAlister, Melani. *Epic Encounters: Culture, Media, and U.S. Interests in the Middle East, 1945–2000*. Berkeley: University of California Press, 2001.
———. "One Black Allah: The Middle East in the Cultural Politics of African American Liberation, 1955–1970." *American Quarterly* 51, no. 3 (September 1999): 622–56.
McBee, Cecil. Interview with author. Maine, July 2001. Tape and transcript in author's possession.
Michel, Ed. Telephone interview with author. May 2001. Tape and transcript in author's possession.
Monson, Ingrid. *Freedom Sounds: Civil Rights Call Out to Jazz and Africa*. New York: Oxford University Press, 2007.
———."The Problem with White Hipness: Race, Gender, and Cultural Conceptions in Jazz Historical Discourse." *Journal of the American Musicological Society* 48, no. 3 (Autumn 1995): 396–442.
Mukenge, Ida Rousseau. *The Black Church in Urban America: A Case Study in Political Economy*. Lanham, Md.: University Press of America, 1983.
Murray, Albert. *Stomping the Blues*. New York: McGraw-Hill, 1976.
Neal, Larry. *Visions of a Liberated Future: Black Arts Movement Writings*. New York: Thunder's Mouth, 1989.
Niebuhr, H. Richard. *The Social Sources of Denominationalism*. New York: Holt, 1929.
Norris, Shanti. Telephone interview with author. August 2003. Tape and transcript in author's possession.
Padoux, André. *Vac: The Concept of the Word in Selected Hindu Tantras*. Translated by Jacques Gontier. Albany: State University of New York Press, 1990.
Panken, Ted. "Detroit Files." *Down Beat* 67, no. 10 (2000): 44–49.
Porter, Lewis. *John Coltrane: His Life and Music*. Ann Arbor: University of Michigan Press, 1998.
Prashad, Vijay. *The Karma of Brown Folk*. Minneapolis: University of Minnesota Press, 2000.
Ramsey, Guthrie, Jr. *Race Music: Black Cultures from Bebop to Hip-Hop*. Berkeley: University of California Press, 2003.
Reagon, Bernice Johnson. *If You Don't Go, Don't Hinder Me: The African American Sacred Song Tradition*. Lincoln: University of Nebraska Press, 2001.
———. *We'll Understand It Better by and by: Pioneering African American Gospel Composers*. Washington: Smithsonian Institute Press, 1992.
Reyes-Botafasina, Radha. Interview with author. Agoura Hills, Calif., June 2007. Tape and transcript in author's possession.
Ricks, George Robinson. "Some Aspects of the Religious Music of the United States Negro: An Ethnomusicological Study with Special Emphasis on the Gospel Tradition." Ph.D. diss., Northwestern University, 1960.
Roof, Wade Clark. *Spiritual Marketplace: Babyboomers and the Remaking of American Religion*. Princeton, N.J.: Princeton University Press, 1999.
Shogan, Robert, and Tom Craig. *The Detroit Riot: A Study in Violence*. Philadelphia: Chilton, 1964.

Sidran, Ben. *Black Talk.* New York: Holt, Rinehart and Winston, 1971.
Slobin, Mark. *Subcultural Sounds: Micromusics of the West.* Middletown, Conn.: Wesleyan University Press, 1993.
Smitherman, Geneva. *Talkin and Testifyin: The Language of Black America.* Detroit: Wayne State University Press, 1986.
Southern, Eileen. "Hymnals of the Black Church." *The Black Perspective in Music* 17, no. 1 (1986): 153–70.
——. *The Music of Black Americans.* 2nd ed. New York: Norton, 1983.
Spencer, Jon Michael. *Black Hymnody: A Hymnological History of the African-American Church.* Knoxville: University of Tennessee Press, 1992.
Such, David Glen. *Avant-Garde Jazz Musicians: Performing "Out There."* Iowa City: University of Iowa Press, 1993.
Sugrue, Thomas J. *The Origins of the Urban Crisis: Race and Inequality in Postwar Detroit.* Princeton, N.J.: Princeton University Press, 1996.
Szwed, John. *Space Is the Place: The Lives and Times of Sun Ra.* New York: Pantheon, 1997.
Taylor, Charles. *The Ethics of Authenticity.* Cambridge, Mass.: Harvard University Press, 1992.
Tell Me How Long Trane's Been Gone. Radio documentary produced by Steve Rowland and written by Larry Abrams. 5 CDs. Chicago: WFMT Fine Arts Network, 2001.
Thurman, Howard. *With Head and Heart: The Autobiography of Howard Thurman.* New York: Harcourt Brace Jovanovich, 1979.
Tipton, Steven M. *Getting Saved from the Sixties.* Berkeley: University of California Press, 1981.
Toop, David. "Alice Coltrane: Universal Consciousness." *Wire*, no. 221 (July 2002): 37–44.
Turner, Richard Brent. *Islam in the African American Experience.* Bloomington: Indiana University Press, 1997.
Tynan, Josh. "India's Master Musician." *Down Beat* 32, no. 10 (1965): 14–16.
Unterbrink, Mary. *Jazz Women at the Keyboard.* Jefferson, N.C.: McFarland, 1983.
Walker, Alice. *In Search of Our Mother's Gardens: Womanist Prose.* 1967. Reprint, San Diego, Calif.: Harcourt Brace Jovanovich, 1982.
Wallace, Michelle. "A Black Feminist's Search for Sisterhood." In *All the Women Are White, All the Blacks Are Men, but Some of Us Are Brave: Black Women's Studies*, edited by Gloria T. Hull, Patricia Bell Scott, and Barbara Smith, 5–13. New York: Feminist Press, 1982.
Washington, Joseph R., Jr. *Black Religion: The Negro Christianity in the United States.* Boston: Beacon, 1964.
Weinstein, Norman C. *A Night in Tunisia: Imaginings of Africa in Jazz.* Metuchen, N.J.: Scarecrow, 1992.
Wilmore, Gayraud S. *Black Religion and Black Radicalism: An Interpretation of the Religious History of Afro-Americans.* 3rd ed. Maryknoll, N.Y.: Orbis, 1998.
Wilson, Olly. "The Heterogeneous Sound Ideal in African-American Music." In

Signifyin(g), Sanctifyin' and Slam Dunking, edited by Gena Dagel Caponi, 157–71. Amherst: University of Massachusetts Press, 1992.
Wood, Vishnu. Interview with author. Springfield, Mass., October 2001. Tape and transcript in author's possession.
Wuthnow, Robert. *After Heaven: Spirituality in America Since the 1950s.* Berkeley: University of California Press, 1998.
———. *Experimentation in American Religion: The New Mysticisms and Their Implications for the Churches*. Berkeley: University of California Press, 1978.
Yogananda, Paramahansa. *Autobiography of a Yogi.* 1946. Reprint, Los Angeles: Self Realization Fellowship, 1979.

Discography

COLTRANE, ALICE

A Monastic Trio. Recorded January 1968. LP. 1968. Impulse!
Huntington Ashram Monastery. Recorded May 14, 1969. LP. 1969. Impulse!
Ptah the El Daoud. Recorded January 26, 1970. LP. 1970. Impulse!
Journey in Satchidananda. Recorded November 8, 1970. LP. 1970. Impulse!
Universal Consciousness. Recorded 1971. LP. 1971. Impulse!
World Galaxy. Recorded November 1971. LP. 1971. Impulse!
Lord of Lords. Recorded July 1972. LP. 1972. Impulse!
Illuminations. With Carlos Santana. LP. 1974. CBS.
Eternity. Recorded August 1975. LP. 1975. Warner Brothers.
Transcendence. Recorded May 1977. LP. 1977. Warner Brothers.
Radha Krsna Nama Sankirtana. Recorded August 1977. LP. 1977. Warner Brothers.
Transfiguration. Recorded live at Shoenberg Hall, the University of California at Los Angeles, April 16, 1978. LP. 1978. Warner Brothers.
Turiya Sings. Cassette. 1982. Avatar Book Institute.
Divine Songs. Cassette. 1987. Avatar Book Institute.
Infinite Chants. Cassette. 1991 Avatar Book Institute.
Glorious Chants. CD. 1995. Avatar Book Institute.
Translinear Light. CD. 2003. Impulse!

COLTRANE, JOHN

Africa Brass. 1961. LP. Impulse!
Ascension. LP. 1965. Impulse!
A Love Supreme. LP. 1965. Impulse!
Om. Recorded October 1965. LP. 1965. Impulse!
Meditations. Recorded November 1965. LP. 1966. Impulse!

COLTRANE, JOHN, AND ALICE COLTRANE

Live at the Village Vanguard Again! Recorded May 28, 1966. LP. 1980. Impulse!
Live in Japan. Tracks 1–3 recorded live at Shinjuku Kosei Nenkin Hall, Tokyo, July 11, 1966; tracks 4–6 recorded live at Shankei Hall, Tokyo, July 22, 1966. LP. 1966. Impulse!
Stellar Regions. Recorded February 15, 1967. LP. 1995. Impulse!
Expression. Recorded February and March 1967. LP. 1993. MCA.
The Olatunji Concert: The Last Live Recording. Recorded April 1967. CD. 2001. Impulse!
Cosmic Music. Recorded 1966–68. LP. 1968. Impulse!

GIBBS, TERRY

Jewish Melodies in Jazztime. Recorded January 11 and 12, 1963. LP. 1963. Mercury.
The Family Album. Recorded February 19, 1963. LP. 1963. Damil.
El Nutto. LP. 1964. Mercury.

HENDERSON, JOE

The Elements. Recorded October 1973. LP. 1996. Milestone.

TYNER, MCCOY

Extensions. LP. 1970. Blue Note.

Index

MUSIC/CULTURE

A series from Wesleyan University Press

Edited by Harris M. Berger and Annie J. Randall

Originating editors: George Lipsitz, Susan McClary, and Robert Walser

Listening to Salsa: Gender, Latin Popular Music, and Puerto Rican Cultures
by Frances Aparicio

Jazz Consciousness: Music, Race, and Humanity
by Paul Austerlitz

Metal, Rock, and Jazz: Perception and the Phenomenology Musical Experience
by Harris M. Berger

Identity and Everyday Life: Essays in the Study of Folklore, Music, and Popular Culture
by Harris M. Berger and Giovanna P. Del Negro

Monument Eternal: The Music of Alice Coltrane
by Franya J. Berkman

Bright Balkan Morning: Romani Lives and the Power of Music in Greek Macedonia
by Dick Blau and Charles and Angeliki Keil

Musical Childhoods and the Cultures of Youth
edited by Susan Boynton and Roe-Min Kok

Music and Cinema
edited by James Buhler, Caryl Flinn, and David Neumeyer

My Music
by Susan D. Crafts, Daniel Cavicchi, Charles Keil, and the Music in Daily Life Project

Born in the USA: Bruce Springsteen and the American Tradition
by Jim Cullen

Presence and Pleasure: The Funk Grooves of James Brown and Parliament
by Anne Danielsen

Echo and Reverb: Fabricating Space in Popular Music Recording, 1900–1960
by Peter Doyle

Recollecting from the Past: Musical Practice and Spirit Possession on the East Coast of Madagascar
by Ron Emoff

Locating East Asia in Western Art Music
edited by Yayoi Uno Everett and Frederick Lau

Black Rhythms of Peru: Reviving African Musical Heritage in the Black Pacific
by Heidi Feldman

"You Better Work!" Underground Dance Music in New York City
by Kai Fikentscher

The Hidden Musicians Music-Making in an English Town
by Ruth Finnegan

The Other Side of Nowhere: Jazz, Improvisation, and Communities in Dialogue
edited by Daniel Fischlin and Ajay Heble

Empire of Dirt: The Aesthetics and Rituals of British "Indie" Music
by Wendy Fonarow

The 'Hood Comes First:
Race, Space, and Place in Rap and Hip-Hop
by Murray Forman

Wired for Sound:
Engineering and Technologies in Sonic Cultures
edited by Paul D. Greene and Thomas Porcello

Sensational Knowledge:
Embodying Culture Through Japanese Dance
by Tomie Hahn

Voices in Bali:
Energies and Perceptions in Vocal Music and Dance Theater
by Edward Herbst

Traveling Spirit Masters:
Moroccan Gnawa Trance and Music in the Global Marketplace
by Deborah Kapchan

Symphonic Metamorphoses:
Subjectivity and Alienation in Mahler's Re-Cycled Songs
by Raymond Knapp

Umm Kulthūm:
Artistic Agency and the Shaping of an Arab Legend, 1967–2007
Laura Lohman

A Thousand Honey Creeks Later:
My Life in Music from Basie to Motown—and Beyond
by Preston Love

Music and Technoculture
edited by René T.A. Lysloff and Leslie C. Gay, Jr.

Songs, Dreamings, and Ghosts:
The Wangga of North Australia
by Allan Marett

Phat Beats, Dope Rhymes:
Hip Hop Down Under Comin' Upper
by Ian Maxwell

Some Liked It Hot:
Jazz Women in Film and Television, 1928–1959
By Kristin A. McGee

Carriacou String Band Serenade:
Performing Identity in the Eastern Caribbean
by Rebecca S. Miller

Global Noise:
Rap and Hip-Hop outside the USA
edited by Tony Mitchell

Popular Music in Theory:
An Introduction
by Keith Negus

Upside Your Head!
Rhythm and Blues on Central Avenue
by Johnny Otis

Coming to You Wherever You Are:
MuchMusic, MTV, and Youth Identities
by Kip Pegley

Singing Archaeology:
Philip Glass's Akhnaten
by John Richardson

Black Noise:
Rap Music and Black Culture in Contemporary America
by Tricia Rose

The Book of Music and Nature:
An Anthology of Sounds, Words, Thoughts
edited by David Rothenberg and Marta Ulvaeus

Angora Matta:
Fatal Acts of North-South Translation
by Marta Elena Savigliano

Making Beats:
The Art of Sample-Based Hip-Hop
by Joseph G. Schloss

Dissonant Identities:
The Rock 'n' Roll Scene in Austin, Texas
by Barry Shank

Among the Jasmine Trees:
Music and Modernity in Contemporary Syria
by Jonathan Holt Shannon

Banda:
Mexican Musical Life across Borders
by Helena Simonett

Global Soundtracks:
Worlds of Film Music
edited by Mark Slobin

Subcultural Sounds:
Micromusics of the West
by Mark Slobin

Music, Society, Education
by Christopher Small

Musicking:
The Meanings of Performing and Listening
by Christopher Small

Music of the Common Tongue:
Survival and Celebration
in African American Music
by Christopher Small

Singing Our Way to Victory:
French Cultural Politics and Music
During the Great War
by Regina M. Sweeney

Setting the Record Straight:
A Material History of Classical Recording
by Colin Symes

False Prophet:
Fieldnotes from the Punk Underground
by Steven Taylor

Any Sound You Can Imagine:
Making Music/Consuming Technology
by Paul Théberge

Club Cultures:
Music, Media and Sub-cultural Capital
by Sarah Thornton

Dub:
Songscape and Shattered Songs
in Jamaican Reggae
by Michael E. Veal

Running with the Devil:
Power, Gender, and Madness
in Heavy Metal Music
by Robert Walser

Manufacturing the Muse:
Estey Organs and Consumer Culture
in Victorian America
by Dennis Waring

The City of Musical Memory:
Salsa, Record Grooves, and Popular Culture in
Cali, Colombia
by Lise A. Waxer

ABOUT THE AUTHOR

Franya J. Berkman is an assistant professor of music at Lewis & Clark College.